Your Mastery

- Live it Now!

Based on the "11 Alignment" Telechannel Series

Channeled Teachings and Wisdom

from "US" (United Souls of Heaven and Earth)

Through

Judith Onley

This book and the Mp3s of the telechannels may be
purchased at:

www.judithonley.com

Cover Design: Ann Bennett (Irristible Marketing) and Marsha Pace
Cover Photo: Janice Smith
Interior Design: Marsha Pace (Imagine Designs)
Edited By: Carolyn Gorman and Marsha Pace

PRINTED IN CANADA
Transcontinental Inc.
February 2011
September 2011

Spirituality/Channeling/Inspiration

Dance With Spirit

ISBN 978-0-9868454-0-6

Table of Contents

Dedication

This book is written in honor of those seeking greater awareness, to all who are on a spiritual path and are ready for the next level. This is dedicated to the ones who feel there is more than we consciously know and are willing to seek the truth of who they really are; to be the bright shining lights that live here on earth at this moment in time and to share that light.

~.~.~.~.~.~.~.~.~

"Once prepared, our Divine Self will finally be given the opportunity to emerge triumphant and fly through the human experience with grace and ease, well earned abundance, love that never leaves and support that never lets you down.

Imagine!"

Maureen Moss

www.maureenmoss.com
www.worldpuja.org

(From her book "Commitment to Love: Transforming Human Nature into Divine Nature")

~.~.~.~.~.~.~.~.~

Acknowledgements

To all of those who knew the importance of this work and the alignments of energy that were happening on the 11th of each month. Those who felt without necessarily understanding why, that they had to be on the call with "US" and bring their beautiful presence to the group.

I want to give a special thanks to Julie Heyman. She always saw things from the higher perspective and reflected that back to me when I had my doubts. She hosted me in her home in Ojai for a number of the teleconferences. That allowed an even greater amplification of the energy being that Ojai is an energetic portal. And a very special mention to Placido, her very "in tune" cat who knew when a telechannel was going to happen and would not leave the house until it was over, even when I was facilitating it from somewhere other than Ojai. He is the living example of being a Master that we can all learn from.

To Carolyn Gorman for her assistance with editing. Her support and expertise were invaluable in the process of refining the content to be clear and concise. Also to Carol Comerford and Marsha Pace for their support of the editing and design process. They all so get what this work is about. To Cork Millner for his humor, encouragement, editing and sharing his expertise as an accomplished author.

To Terri Pepin, my original webmaster for all her technical expertise and encouragement. She got me over the hump of feeling overwhelmed with the "how to's" of getting this beautiful information to the public in a timely, easy and joyous way.

Note to Readers

The messages you are about to read are as close to the original transmission as possible because embedded within the words, the patterning, cadence and flow of the sentences is a harmonic coding.

So, I invite you to let go of punctuation rules and simply allow yourself to feel the beautiful vibration.

If you listen to the audio recordings of the channels you will hear clicking, clapping and tapping sounds. This is "US" working through me clearing energy by having me snap my fingers, clap my hands and tap my body in different places.

Much energy work is being done with each of you through the words and sounds whether you were there in person or reading or listening to the channels at a later date. It is all in the "now" moment and you will receive the energy and activation whenever you read or listen to these empowering messages.

. . . Judith

Introduction – Who is "US"?

"US" (United Souls of Heaven and Earth) is a group of loving, supportive non-physical spiritual teachers whose purpose for coming forth at this time is just as their name indicates:

**"To unite heaven and earth
by activating the Divine Essence
within all Human Beings."**

Their wisdom and teachings are timely as we go through the Great Shift and our own personal "spiritual awakening." The words spoken in the channels are not only empowering messages, but activations of our light at very deep cellular levels. This allows us as human beings to "feel" our Divine Essence from within and thereby integrate it fully into our every thought, word and action in our daily lives here on this earth, creating heaven on earth here and now!

Their vibration is of true joy and love intensely felt by all who have been in their presence. They offer us this experience within our physical bodies so that we can remember it for ourselves.

Preface – Author's Notes

The "11 Alignment" teleconference channel series began as guidance
I received from "US" to gather people on the 11th of each month
during 2009. When the number 2009 is added up, it equals eleven.
In the study of numerology, eleven is a "Master number." Master
numbers carry a strong vibration that offer us more awareness of what
is happening around us. This awareness is the catalyst for greater
learning and assimilation of energies and vibration of the Oneness
and our relationship to that Oneness as we move out of the vibration
of duality.

The purpose for gathering people on the teleconferences was to provide
information that would facilitate the anchoring of this "Mastery"
energy through the body for use in our everyday lives: to think,
speak and act as a Master. The gatherings provide an awareness of an
alignment to universal/cosmic energy that humanity is now receiving.
When conscious of that alignment, we are able to amplify the energy
for greater and more beneficial application in our lives, thereby
creating more ease and grace. As a result, we experience much less
struggle because it connects us with the truth within that "knows" no
boundaries or limitations to our true magnificence and our power.

The first channel on January 11th was interesting as I forgot to turn on
the digital voice recorder, so there was no audio version of the original
channel. I had to request the participants on the call to send me notes
on what they heard. (I do not remember the words when I channel. It is
more like being in a dream for me and dissipates quickly afterward). I
am always filled with joy and awe to hear what I channeled and to apply
the words and activations in my own life as well.

We always have a discussion after each channel where participants
share their experiences. Even though what everyone shares is quite
individual, invariably it stimulates someone else's awareness that
something similar was happening for them. As they talk about it, the
energy and knowing is anchored for the group as a whole.

Thankfully, my friend Marlow in British Columbia was able to compile
the responses we received from the participants and put it all together
in a cohesive and comprehensive version of the original channel, so it

will read a bit differently than the other channels.

Each month, the channel has its own theme and flavour and feels very empowering as you read it. You will actually feel the energy as though you were right there during the teleconference. "US" is able to communicate their wisdom in such loving, supportive and interesting ways across time as we see it. They are truly Masters.

We have come to a point right now that is unprecedented in history. This is a time when we, the human family, are opening up to a new level of awareness, consciousness and sensitivity and are freely participating in our unique spiritual evolution.

This series of channeled teachings serve to describe and communicate the changing nature of our times. They are presented here in order to shed light on some of the tumult of the dynamic year 2009. We are ever reminded that all is in accordance with the Divine Plan and that each of us has a unique and pivotal role to play in its unfoldment. This book brings you clarity on what that role is for you.

Be aware of the feeling of the vibrations as you start to read each channel. After you have read the book completely, I suggest you go back and reread each channel one at a time, then just sit with it as you integrate the message into your energy field and awareness. As you reread the words (or listen to the audio recordings) repeatedly, you will absorb the alignment at a deeper cellular level. You will be giving your body the "physical" experience of what it feels like to be Divine and the more often you can do that, the more it becomes the default or automatic pilot program that you operate from. Instead of operating from the common feelings of denseness and fear, your life becomes a JOYFUL journey that you will look forward to each day.

I encourage you to also experience listening to the telechannels. To order the Mp3s go to www.dancewithspirit.com .

I am grateful and honored to have "US" as a presence in my life. I move forward with complete trust and knowing that we are all to be of service in ways that we could not ever have imagined!

. . . *Judith*

Invocation

(This is the invocation I use every time I am with a group, on a telechannel, or with a person in a private session to center us and call in "US." As soon as we start the breaths, it takes us out of our mind and into our body. I feel the shift of energy and the knowing of the presence of "US." This is the experience that "US" is here to facilitate: to feel our Divine Essence within our body. So as you read these words, or listen to them on the audio recordings, notice when you feel the shift of energy and are aware of the loving presence of "US.")

Take three really deep breaths. These three breaths connect body, mind, and Spirit.

And when the three work in harmony with each other, they create a state of well-being and a sense of inner peace.

And it is from this place of inner peace that ALL is possible:

Your physical well-being . . .

Your mental clarity . . .

Your emotional balance . . .

And your Spiritual knowing . . .

Now as you breathe in, allow yourself to connect to that beautiful Divine Essence of who you are, that place deep inside that only knows love, joy, health, empowerment, (fill in with any other intentions you have) and inner knowing.

And as you breathe out, just let go, and ALLOW.

Let go of any old belief systems, thought patterns, conditioning and behaviors that are no longer serving you.

Let go of the denser energies of fear, doubt, worry, guilt (add any others that may apply to you).

Embrace them knowing that they have served you, and then literally see them dissolve and float right out of your mind, out of your body, and right out of your energy field. As these denser energies leave, they create an empty space, a void that can now be filled up with higher vibrational energy. The energy of the truth of who you are in all of your glory and magnificence.

So as you breathe in, just allow yourself to FEEL what it feels like from the inside!

~.~.~.~.~.~.~.~.~.~.~.~.

January 11 - Allowing Newness
(Robert's Creek, BC)

(This is an annotated version of the channeling that was received on January 11, 2009, during the teleconference channel. Since the session was not recorded in its usual fashion, the text below is a compilation of the notes of those who participated in the event and what I remembered from the channel. For those of you who did have an opportunity to hear the material first hand, we hope that this serves as a reminder and for those of you who were not present, we trust that what is presented here is of service in your continued unfoldment!

I have listed the key points in bullet form followed by some comments and reflections the participants had subsequent to the actual transmission.)

In summation, we must BE the Light . . .

- Where there is light, darkness cannot reside. It's easier than ever to keep your vibration high or create more light and from there all is possible; answers and guidance come.

- A new story is being written. It must come through you. You are creating the new world. It is a co-creation. As you receive messages from "US," send those messages back out. Be open to new people and situations. Be open-minded and open-hearted to people and situations that are different from you. You are creating strength from within your Core Divinity.

- Old patterns and beliefs are dissolving with the breath from the new energy. This energy is not like anything before, so there is nowhere in history that you can go back to and look upon to get guidance on how to use this energy. There is no reference point.

- You are clearing density so the light can come in. Exude your light to new experiences and opportunities. Sit in the center and energy will be projected out; it is not on the outside.

- There will be lots of physical clearings and accelerated energies. Many of the discomforts and pains that have been experienced are a result of this clearing to give spiritual, emotional, and physical strength. Moon energy helps move emotions. The physical pain that many have experienced over the two weeks post Solstice period has been a result of tremendous clearing and dissolving.

- Keep your vibration high. Let go of attachment to how outcomes are supposed to look. TRUST!

- Through a sense of empowerment you create new experiences. It starts with each one of you; within you. Ask what the next experience will be and it will unfold. Allow your own creation. Choose which new experience serves you best. "Eleven" is creating the energy of newness. Allow openness and newness into your lives. You are a wayshower, empowerer and Lightworker.

- Exude your light to those you haven't even met yet. Don't discount any possibilities. It's "to you" and "through you," never one way. There is a wealth of wisdom in new experiences for the new earth. Sit in your inner realm to connect to these experiences. Like a movie inside coming through you to the outer world, it is YOU designing the new world. This is a time of co-creation, with helpers empowering each other, back and forth to you from Spirit and returning through you to Spirit.

- The light that you radiate comes from your Beingness. It is not a function of what you say or do; it is demonstrated in the way that you show up for things.

- Step out, no hiding! There will be new people in your life. It may not be how or what you think. Take ownership of your Mastery.

- You are entering a time of unprecedented opportunities for new experience. You are counseled to say "YES!" to whatever presents itself and are being invited to step into totally new challenges, relationships and explorations. It doesn't matter how they "seem" to be, it's all good, because new avenues of experience and expression are being initiated. There are new people to meet and jobs and places to explore.

- Stay centerd in your own stillness even though it looks as though the world around you is falling apart or even exploding. Be assured that these are the old, outmoded structures fracturing and allowing new forms to come into being. This is true on governmental, monetary, structural, earthly and relationship levels.

- The blades of the airplanes' propeller are always solid and real; it is only the change in frequency and vibration that seems to make them disappear. When it is spinning so fast, one cannot even SEE it. This relates to how things are (or can be) for some people. There are negative things around them but they are vibrating differently, so they don't even SEE them! You are like the propellers, solid. As you shift your vibration and consciousness, you vibrate higher (oscillate faster) and will no longer "see" the same things and by extension, will no longer "be seen" by those in the old or denser, slower frequency. You will no longer see the drama and violence in the world around you. You will send a high vibration into issues to break up density and see through it to gain clarity and strength in physical, mental and emotional planes.

- You are altering your own frequency. You may become invisible to some and some will become invisible to you as you move "out of sync" with the old vibration.

- Is your Divinity grounded between heaven and earth supporting others with this strength? You can co-create so much! Share new experiences with each other to assist change. How can you better shift into the new world? On the highest level of your being, nothing is done "to you" or "for you." You create your world. You cannot base it on any old ways. Many more alignments are coming soon.

- Time to stand in the Light and know that you are the ones that you have been waiting for.

Here are a few of the comments that were shared by some of the participants during the discussion afterward:

"It seems easier to connect with either my Higher Self, or Higher Beings, letting go of ego and aligning with the Universal Energy and perhaps God's Will. I remember feeling a sense of excitement after the channeling that 'All Is Possible' and all we need to do is 'Trust!' That seems to be the message (for me anyhow) of the year. I really feel it's a year of connection with the Higher Will of all concerned and trusting that I and my needs and desires will be looked after. Don't know if this is of any help to you, but it sure helped me this morning to share that. Thank You!"
Shannon C., British Columbia

"It is ME designing the new world, co-creating together with helpers empowering each other, back and forth to you and returning through you to me. We are becoming teachers by our experiences and to be willing to share in love, joy, dance and music."
Phyllis W., British Columbia

"I loved when "US" was referring to a guidance they gave Judith when she was flying back to British Columbia recently as she looked outside the plane and noticed that though she knew the propellers on the plane were solid and three dimensional, as they spun faster and faster, by virtue of their frequency of revolution, they appeared to be invisible. The awareness that was being shown through this observation was that there is much that we have not been able to see that we will now be able to because we are vibrating at a higher frequency and that made sense to me."
Marlow P., British Columbia

"It is like an amusement park ride, it scares us but we cannot wait to get back on it. Low vibrational experiences are being replaced with new higher vibrational thoughts and experiences. We are no longer seeing lower levels of density. We need to shut down the old in order to embrace the new. We may be learning to feel in a different way. We are channeling the energy. We are conduits."
Barbara L., Ontario

"US" talked about meeting people now and in the future once we are in our joy and living in the present moment and how we connect with people etherically. Telepathy will be our future as human angels in many years to come once we are rid of the old way of talking to communicate our ideas. "US" also talked about how language is limiting and not equal to the task of sharing and communicating the new energies or their messages. This will make manifesting our dreams faster. We will not have the old paradigms with us but will have shifted into the new energies of the new earth."
Kevin N., Ontario

(Judith would like to thank Shannon, Phyllis, Barbara, Kevin and Marlow for offering their notes, thoughts and transcription.)

~.~.~.~.~.~.~.~.~.~.~.

February 11 - Being Open to Receive
(Oakdale, CA)

Dear Beautiful Beings of Light,

We are the United Souls of Heaven and of Earth. It always brings us great delight to be in the midst of a group of human beings who are so dedicated to their path of knowing, of allowing, of being open to more, to more than their eyes can see or to be in that place of allowing what they are feeling from the inside.

So we are in great honor and in great awe of each of you as you choose to take the next step in your awareness, in your openness to know more of the truth of who you are.

And that is the purpose for us coming forth at this time: to share our words and our wisdom through our host. And through our energy to you, to help you to really have an experience of knowing that truth about yourself, that truth that you are a Divine Being in a human body, having a human and a combination of spiritual experiences.

As you evolve as a spirit, as a soul and as a human being all wrapped up in one package, this is where it gets very confusing for most of you because you have been taught that it is only about the 3D realm, the very physical realm where you can see and touch and taste and smell something. And now it is about more of your senses opening up, more of your awareness of things that are non-tangible, that are just felt or experienced or possibly just a deep inner knowing and we again honor you for trusting that because that will take you far. (Pause)

And we always take a pause to allow that information, our words to filter from your mind through your body, through your heart, so that you get it at a very deep cellular level; have that experience of knowing that truth, that truth that is already a part of you. We are not saying anything new, we are just helping you to remember that truth, to help to activate it so you feel it more on a daily basis, that you do not have to just be out of your body go into meditation or to have a mystical experience to know that wonderful feeling of love, of joy, of harmony and of peace from within. Because, Dear Ones, it is already there for you. It always has been. It always will be. And as you accept that part of yourself, that unseen part that there are no words to describe, it is not tangible, you cannot touch it, but you definitely can feel it. (Pause)

And again we take that pause because it is about feeling it, not thinking it, not knowing it, about truly feeling it in your body. You are in a physical body. Your spirit is integrated with the physical body and you are raising the vibration of this physical body. You can actually have more experiences of that harmony from within, that peace from within.

So Dear Ones, it is at a time of great acceleration that you all come together and we always love the discussions at the beginning that you share with our host because when you do that you are actually activating that for yourself. When you talk about that knowing and that feeling and that calling, that is what is happening for you. You are acknowledging it so in the acknowledging of that, by taking an action now to fulfill that, you have made a great leap in your acceleration, in your evolution, in your personal growth and in your spiritual growth and we honor you for that.

We are here to help facilitate but we cannot do it for anybody as our host cannot do anything. All of you who are in any kind of what you would call metaphysical healing spiritual work are very aware that you can facilitate but you cannot do it for another person. You can model it for yourself and have them see that harmony from within you or that inner peace, but it is really a conscious choice on each individuals' part to embody that for themselves, to always make a choice to come back to that point of that inner knowing and that trusting from within.

It is possible for you in each moment and as you have each experience build upon each next experience, it is the new programming that is happening for you. The old programming is actually getting deleted and these are words that we again are saying to you so that your mind can understand that there is much shifting happening. There is a de-programming and a re-programming and a re-wiring and a re-calibration happening to you on a very consistent basis now energetically and that is what you are experiencing. So if you are able to just trust and allow, it will be a much more graceful and easy experience.

If you allow yourself to question or be in fear around it or to struggle with it or resist, it will be a longer process for you and much less joyful. So we are here to help you at this time to facilitate that feeling of joy from within. (Pause)

Again we take a pause to allow those words, that information, that energy to filter down through your mind and through your body and to really experience that in your heart center.

It is time, Dear Ones, for you to experience the joy of your life. You have, you know what the struggles are, you know what the challenges are, and it is now time to truly accept, allow, be open to, and to receive the joy. There is nothing wrong with that. You have been told that you have to work hard. You have been told that you always have to give, give, give. You have been told that you do this wrong and that wrong and yes, you may need to make some different choices. It doesn't mean that they're right or they're wrong.

It is now about standing in that center and feeling your own joy, and creating that in each moment, to feeling your own love and to experience that and to be able to give that. And for most of you, for those of you who have chosen to be part of this group today, it isn't even about giving it. You are all wonderful givers. Because you are constantly giving and that is where you are experiencing your joys, in the giving, it is now time for each and every one of you to take a step back, to take a breath and to allow yourselves to receive.

And again we feel that energy. It kind of triggers some of you because you are not used to receiving. You are not even sure how to go about that or how to ask for that. And there are some of you in this group that are gradually learning that that is possible and when you take that leap and that trust, you actually ask for something, you are very astounded at how easy it is that people will respond to you and it is a gift that you are actually giving them to be able to give back to you.

And it is a message that we have spoken of many times in previous channels that giving and receiving is a two-way flow. The moment it starts only going one way, whether it is always a giving or for some people they think they are always needing to receive, it becomes out of balance. So it is a time right now in your spiritual evolution as human beings in the 3D realm to find that balance of giving, of receiving, of male, of female, of right, of wrong, of all of the things that have felt like opposites so that there is a flow, that beautiful flow that happens with ease and with grace.

So take a moment to take a breath and feel that from within you, to feel that ebb and flow that happens. It is never always one thing, you are never always on a high or never always on a low, you are never always right or never always wrong in your perception. There is always a shifting of energies and just allow yourself to tune in right now to that giving and through that receiving of energy. So as you listen to our words, your ears are receiving and, if you allow your hearts to be open, we are able to send you much love. (Pause)

Again we take the pause so that you can feel that energy not just hear the words, but actually to feel the energy within your body and it is the opening of the heart that is creating the shift in your world that true sense of deep love from within and as you allow yourselves to be loved in whatever form that may be. It might just be someone smiling at you, it might be someone giving you a very thoughtful gift, it might be someone giving you a kind word or just picking up the phone and saying, "I was thinking about you today." Or it might be something really huge that somebody has done to really support you. It is about you acknowledging that, that you are, Dear Ones, worth it, deserving, and capable of receiving, that this energy of love, of support, is there for all of you. It is there in your interconnections with each other.

There are people poised who are just waiting at this moment that we speak to give to you. It is their nature. It is their purpose. It is their calling. And it is time now to be in that opening of receiving and that is our message to you.

We have spoken before about giving and receiving and that two-way flow and that importance but the message to this group and, as our host said, you came together for a very specific reason. It is about the vibration of being open to receiving and asking for what you want.

Our host had individual discussions with many of you around that topic and so we are delighted to be able to work with the energy of that, to help it to assimilate and to be activated within your bodies so it does not have to be a mental effort. You do not have to analyze every situation and ask yourself, "Oh wow, should I accept that?" or "Should I ask for that?" or "Should I, should I, should I?" There is no more "should I."

It is just about being and in your beingness, Dear Ones, there will be many forms of energy that are being given to you, in the physical, in the mental, in the emotional, in the spiritual, and in all shapes, sizes, and forms.

If you are in that space of opening to receive, many miracles are happening as we speak. There is an orchestration that is happening in the cosmos and all of the different dimensions of this energy of manifestation, of miracles, of abundance, of health, of many, many things when you stand in that place of affirming, acknowledging, and taking and even commanding. And commanding is not demanding. Commanding is just being in an energy of receiving and of being certain of that receiving; not doubting it, not questioning it, not hoping for it, but literally commanding for that receiving and being open for it to come in to your space, in to your physical space as well as your energetic space.

So that is the message in the energy that we are working with you today, is opening to receive, asking for what you want.

And we are going to repeat this a number of times through this message so that you get it on all levels. It is in the repetition that the re-programming happens. There has been many, many, many years in your lifetime and many eons of patterning that has happened that are now being dissolved and as that is being dissolved you can make a very conscious permission and effort for it to be replaced with what serves you on a much higher level and what serves your humanity, your globe, and the cosmos.

And we have said this before: as you embody that for yourself, as you are open to receive, whether it is the wonderful love and energy from "US" and all of your guides and all of your angelic support, or whether it is opening to receive something very physical from a friend or a family member, it is all the same energy, but it is happening on all levels, not just your physical realm. It is happening on all of the dimensional realms.

There are many spiritual beings, non-physical spiritual beings that are poised at this time to support you as you are evolving and all it takes is the asking. (Pause)

And we pause again to let that filter down to let the uncomfortableness that that triggers in our words for you to be dispelled, for you to really embrace it in your heart. It is okay to ask.

And the trick to being okay with asking is to be detached from the outcome. So when you ask with an agenda or a very specific motive in mind and very attached to what that looks like or the outcome, that is where you cause the disappointment in yourself or possibly in obligation in another, that your world has been so entangled up in. But if you are able to come to that place within yourself that you are comfortable to ask for what it is you want or need, but also to be comfortable whether you receive it or not or in what form you receive it. Because what will happen is it frees the other person or energy that you may be asking from to actually give you something more.

So even possibly if they choose to say "no," it means that you may be getting it from another source that is even grander. Your minds have trouble wrapping themselves around that because you have been taught to live in such limited thinking and limited space and we are here to help support you to open up those possibilities for miracles, great grand miracles that you have no concept of. And when you're in that place of allowing and openness, you will be shown. There will be much come to you that you will shake your head and say, "I would not have believed, I would not even have known to have asked for this," but just to be open now to the allowing of the receiving.

Dear Ones, as you open your hearts to receive that energy you will find an inner peace and an excitement within you that then will draw all of these things to you. And again they do not need to be in the material realm, they might be something material, they might be something monetary, but it really is about the underlying energy of whatever that thing is, whether it allows you to feel freedom, whether it allows you to feel love, whether it allows you to feel peace or security, it is never about the thing, it is always about the reason why you want it.

So, often ask yourself when you are in that place of asking, "What is the underlying feeling that you actually want from whatever that is." And that is what you will receive and it may be in a very different form than you expect it to be and that may show up as another person that you may not even expected that they showed up in your life and you may not have been open for it at one time.

As you allow yourself to open to different types of beings and people in your life you will be very amazed and we can hear our host laughing at the comment because she had an experience this week of exactly that of opening up and allowing and this wonderful being came into one of her channels that she would never have expected and had a very different experience around all of that. So it is about the openness to all the possibilities that are there right before you and that are in co-creation with you right at this moment as we speak.

So Dear Ones, we are going to leave you now with that beautiful energy and activation and facilitation for yourselves to be open to receiving by asking for what you want.

We leave you now with great joy in our hearts and honor for you the Divine Beings that you already are and the remembrance of that truth. We leave you now.

~.~.~.~.~.~.~.~.~.~.~.

Key Points:

- *It is now time to truly accept, allow, be open to, and to receive the joy. Because you are constantly giving, that is where you are experiencing your joys, in the giving. It is now time for each and every one of you to take a step back, to take a breath and to allow yourselves to receive.*

- *If you are in that space of opening to receive, many miracles are happening. There is an orchestration that is happening in the cosmos and all of the different dimensions of this energy of manifestation, of miracles, of abundance, of health, of many, many things when you stand in that place of affirming, acknowledging, and taking and even commanding.*

- *Commanding is not demanding. Commanding is just being in an energy of receiving and of being certain of that receiving; not doubting it, not questioning it, not hoping for it, but literally commanding for that receiving and being open for it to come in to your space, in to your physical space as well as your energetic space.*

- *There are many spiritual beings, physical and non-physical spiritual beings that are poised at this time to support you as you are evolving and all it takes is the asking. The trick to being okay with asking is to be detached from the outcome and open up those possibilities for miracles in that place of allowing.*

- *As you open your hearts to receive that energy you will find an inner peace and an excitement within you that will draw all of these things to you. It is never about the thing, it is always about the reason why you want it.*

March 11 - Divine Alignment With Self
(La Mesa, CA)

Dearest Beautiful Beings of Light,

We are the United Souls of Heaven and of Earth and it brings us great joy, great delight to be able to communicate with you through our host at this time, at this place and at this moment.

It is always a Divine alignment when groups, individuals create a group, a group of Lightworkers, of Light Beings, of Spiritual Beings that come together at a certain point in time and it is a Divine alignment and we are here to tell you and to help you feel the relevance and the importance of that.

This timing of Divine alignment was actually spoken of in your introductions and it truly is about the time of NOW! It is a Divine alignment that is happening now and it is accelerating with great speed and great intensity for all of you because it is time. The time is NOW and the Divine alignment is happening whether you are aware of it or not aware of it, it is still happening.

So as you choose to become more conscious and to become more aware of this Divine alignment your path will open up before your very eyes and there will be a dissolving of the struggle because as you become aligned with your Divinity, with your Divine Essence, as all of those parts of you that have been fragmented all over the place come into alignment, come into cooperation with yourself. It is not a matter of coming into cooperation with others.

What you are working on at this time is coming into cooperation with yourself. Not anything or anyone else. It is the Divine alignment with your Divine Essence that is happening for you as we speak. As you go through these great shifts that you spoke of in your introductions, that is what is happening, Dear Ones. You are shifting from being out of alignment with your Divine Self to being in alignment with your Divine Self, all of those aspects. And one of the aspects that we want to address here today with all of you is that aspect of yourself that feels like that you have done something wrong. (Pause)

And we take a pause at this time to allow the energy; the words and the energy to shift from your mind and through your body as that is where you are able to then take action on it, to BE it, to BE that truth of who you are, that Divine Essence.

So, it is about this alignment that is happening with even those parts of yourself that feel like you may have done something wrong. Our host has had discussions with her friends in the last few days about that very energy of feeling like you have done something wrong. Even the sessions she has done with her clients have been about: "There are no mistakes, there are no wrong decisions!" It is only what you have been told or what you have been conditioned to that creates that energy of constriction, because you feel like you have done something wrong.

When you do things from your heart, when you keep moving forward with your guidance, you may not understand why you are having that guidance or why somebody else is having guidance to interact with you in a certain way and it is not until that moment coagulates and happens and the results are seen that you understand why all that has happened.

And this is a very intense aspect that is happening for all of you right now in your spiritual evolution, in your personal evolution, in your human evolution, in your 3D world evolution. There are aspects of yourself that are stepping forward to show you that it is All OKAY! (Pause)

And we take the pause again for that to filter, for the information and energy to filter through your body and into the earth because it is ALL OKAY! Everything that is happening in your life personally, every thought, every word, every action are all the aspects coming together for you in your consciousness and as you make those conscious choices, that is where then you open up to the EASE, to the JOY and to the GRACE.

So as you acknowledge that each decision that you have made has been in your highest good, as well as others highest good, as well as your global and universal highest good, that takes away the judgement. So even though as you look out into your world you see many things that you would want to judge as wrong, we are here to tell you that if you take that energy of wrong out of it, things will transform much quicker. It is judgement that you are holding on yourself, on others and on events in your world that have kept you in a box, that has kept it constricted and now it is at a great opening and as you take away your judgement of these events and energies and opportunities, things will shift much quicker, and that is why they ARE shifting much quicker, is because there are so many of you holding the Light at this time that are able to be in that nonjudgemental place. That is allowing the openings, the beautiful openings for miracles to occur, for miracles in your own personal life, for miracles in your communities and your families, for miracles in your world which then create the miracles in the cosmos.

There was much information given to our host in many events that she has attended recently that have all been about the evolution and the great miracles that are happening universally, not just personally, with each of you, but because they are happening at a microcosmic level with each of you and you are stepping into it and you are owning it and you are being open to the possibilities and the opportunities, you ARE affecting the cosmic and the universal shifts that are happening for ALL, for all of you and all of "US" because we are ONE. There is no you and there is no "US." We are truly all one and we have said this many times to our host and in channels.

So as you embrace that totality of who you are in relation to the ALL, to each and every aspect within your personal world as well as the cosmic and universal world, you will see so many things, magnificent things that you could not possibly comprehend at this time.

And so it is all an opening that is happening and it is happening very, very quickly, if you are ready, if you give permission, if you are open to the possibilities, which so many of you are saying YES to those possibilities, to those miracles, to those opportunities and shifting very quickly out of your fear and your worry and your doubt, and you are getting much support energetically for that possibility, for that shift. You have given permission, you have given intent and now all of those aspects of yourself that are multi-dimensional are coming together in the whole of who you are. (Pause)

Again, we take the pause for you to get it, to get it at a physical level, to get it at a cellular level. All of the aspects of you are coming together in the whole, the whole YOU, the whole Universe, the ALLness, the ONEness. Those are just terms that have rolled off your lips and have been taught in many of the mystery schools and from the great teachers and it is now time to understand the truth of that, to feel that at a cellular, biological level of the ONEness of that wholeness. You do not have to have different aspects or different parts of yourself. It is the coming together of the wholeness, that solidifying of who you are that is happening for you right now, and as you give permission for that, it happens at an even greater intensity and it does not have to be difficult.

When you come together in support of each other for all of you who are going though the great shift, the great shift of the ages that has been predicted since the beginning of the time, and support each other in that harmonic energy of the opening of your heart center, of your beingness to what is happening right now, and letting go of all of those things that you have been taught that are not serving you any longer, there is a great joy, harmony, peace and bliss that you feel within you, and many of you are touching on those throughout your day now, not just when you are in your meditation, not just when you are in a peaceful environment, not just when you have had a joyful moment, but as you go through your day.

That is when you know you are living "wholly" and that word is another word that has been used in many contexts. When you are living "wholly" you feel that in every moment, in every thought and every feeling and every expression, and as you bring all of that wholeness into yourselves and allow those possibilities, it does happen in each moment no matter what each of those moments looks like for yourself, or feels like for yourself, each moment is Divine. It is that Divine alignment that we spoke about at the beginning. That Divine alignment is that wholeness of who you are, your world in relation to your Universe, and the Universe is YOU. It is contained in every cell, in every atom and molecule of your body.

You ARE the Universe.

That is what you are feeling. That is what has created so much confusion because there has been SO much, and now it is coming together. It is collaborating, it is coagulating, it is cooperating, it is creating, and it is many, many things happening all at one. So as you stand within your own Divinity, within your own true core energy, that truth of who you are, you give permission for others to do the same. You are that beacon of Light that then shines on others that then makes it easier for them to come into their Divine alignment, to feel their Divine Essence, to be their Divine Being and then have that influence, that radiation out to others.

So Dear Ones, it is happening. It is happening in each moment, in each thought and each action and as you let go of those judgements and know that as you are guided, as you trust your Divine guidance, each decision is the perfect decision. Each decision, each thought that comes from your heart, when you truly move from your heart, there is nothing that you can do wrong because you are living your truth. Whatever your truth is, allows everyone else in your interconnectedness to live their truth as well, and as all Beings start to live their truth, there is that "wholeness," that "holiness," Spiritual Beingness, that Divinity.

There are so many ways to describe this energy. This is what it is, it is about the Divine Alignment of all of the aspects of you. All the ones that you may have judged as good or bad, or right or wrong, or big or little, or ugly or beautiful, it does not matter what those aspects are, they are all part of your Divine Alignment that are coming into the wholeness of who you are as we speak. So take a deep breath Dear Ones and allow yourself to feel that on the inside.

We have spoken many times about feeling your guidance from the inside. You no longer need to look outside for anything. The outside may be a beautiful reflection of what you are doing on the inside, and that is wonderful to acknowledge, but all of your truth lies on the inside. You have everything you have ever needed, wanted or could ever wish for within you, and as you tap into that on a more consistent basis for your own guidance, for your own answers, and for your reflection of yourself, that is where your power is, that is where your own empowerment lies, and it matters not where you are in your Spiritual path that you are always able to embrace that empowerment and make those conscious choices at those choice points in each second, at each moment, whether it be within a physical event in your life, or whether it be an emotional event or spiritual or mental. When you come from that truth from within, from trusting that guidance from within and allowing the possibilities, all is well. All is well in your world which then reverberates you creating "all is well" in THE world, and in the Universe.

So Dear Ones, as you align with this Divine alignment of the 11th Mastery, the 11th energy of Mastery, allow yourself to check in at such a very deep level that it just IS. It just is who you are, no doubts or questions, it just IS. It is the Divine alignment of the truth of who you are. It is your Divine Essence stepping forward to speak that truth, to live that truth, to exude that truth.

So as we leave you now with those words and the energy, it is with great joy in our hearts, and great honor that we are able to support you, to be part of you because we ARE you. We are you and you are "US," and it is all in Divine alignment. We leave you now.

~.~.~.~.~.~.~.~.~.~.~.

Key Points:

- *It is a Divine alignment that is happening now and it is accelerating with great speed and great intensity for all of you because it is time. As you choose to become more conscious and to become more aware of this Divine alignment your path will open up before your very eyes and there will be a dissolving of the struggle as you become aligned with your Divinity, with your Divine Essence, with those parts of you that have been fragmented all over the place.*

- *What you are working on at this time is coming into cooperation with yourself. Not anything or anyone else. This alignment is happening with even those parts of yourself that feel like you may have done something wrong. There are no mistakes, there are no wrong decisions. When you do things from your heart you understand why all has happened.*

- *There are so many of you holding the Light at this time that are able to be in that nonjudgemental place, that it is allowing the openings, the beautiful openings for miracles to occur, for miracles in your own personal life, for miracles in your communities and your families, for miracles in your world which then create the miracles in the cosmos.*

- *So as you stand within your own Divinity, within your own true core energy, that truth of who you are, you give permission for others to do the same.*

- *As you align with this Divine energy of Mastery, it is your Divine Essence stepping forward to speak that truth, to live that truth, to exude that truth. It just is who you are, no doubts or questions, it just IS.*

April 11 - Empowerment of You
(La Mesa, CA)

Dearest Beautiful Beings of Light,

We are the United Souls of Heaven and of Earth and it brings us great delight and great joy, it is an honor for us to share with you our words, our energy, our love, and our joy.

And it is for you to be able to receive, for you to be able to fill yourself up, for you to be able to embody this energy, this energy of your Divine Essence, this energy of the Cosmos, this energy of the Universe. It is all there for you Dear Ones. Just take a breath in and allow yourselves to be filled up. Filled up with this loving energy, filled up with this joyful energy, filled up with this empowering energy, filled up with this amplified energy, amplified because it is the truth of who you are and as you breathe it in, it expands and becomes greater and greater and greater.

So, Dear Ones, take the moment to breathe that in, to truly, truly feel it inside, in your body not in your mind. It is so important at this time to feel your own Essence; not somebody else's, not something someone has told you, not something you have read in a book. It is about feeling it for yourself, feeling yourself, feeling you inside of you. It is happening as we speak that there is a greater connection for you to you, so it is through our words that we help your mind to understand what that means because it is a rather strange concept to understand to be able to connect you with you, and to understand what that is and to feel it in your body, for you to feel the empowerment of you. (Pause)

And we take that pause, Dear Ones, for the information to filter from your mind to your body. Because it is at that body, that physical, biological, cellular level that you are able to take action. Your mind is just a filter, it is just the computer that is taking in the information. It is your body now living it in the core of your being, that will be able to execute whatever it is that you need to do at this time to feel, to express, to be, to act out that empowerment of YOU. Those are words that are very significant for those that are hearing those words at this time or at any time to feel what that is; the empowerment of YOU, and we stress the "you" part of it, because you think empowerment comes from many, many places, Dear Ones, but it truly comes from YOU. Whether you give your power away, whether you embody it, whether you take it from others, all of that is by YOU. And as you become aware and conscious of that and of the choices that you are making and understanding that it is only you that is facilitating whatever is going on in your life, it becomes a much more powerful and EMpowering circumstance and alternative for you to move forward.

It is an accountability to yourself from yourself, from you to you, that is at this time being facilitated through many external circumstances to show you what is possible. So as you are looking for your empowerment from the outside, many things may happen that may not really align with the truth of who you are, or what you were hoping would unfold, or what you would expect in your life, but as you turn that around and bring the empowerment from the inside, the empowerment of you as you, then it will feel much more aligned, it will feel in harmony with the whole, in harmony with YOU.

And again we are going to keep stressing the "you" because that is what it is about. It is not about "US" and our words and our energy and our activation. It is really about you receiving you, activating you, applying all of these truths for yourself and knowing at a deep cellular level, that this is the truth for you, not anybody else. There are many, many truths. Each person has their own truth, but as you live your own truth, that is your empowerment, Dear Ones. It is the truth of you, as you, for you, by you.

The word empowerment has had much attention through the last few decades of self-help, self-growth, self-empowerment. There are many teachers and Masters and workshops and many things to assist you with understanding what that word empowerment is, and now it is time Dear Ones to take it to the next level of "being" it. (Pause)

And again we take the pause for you to get it at that cellular level, to get it at the biological level, to get it at the heart level. And as you move from those levels there will be no question, it will be as easy as pie, Dear Ones. It just will be. There will be no thinking or planning or having to or should to or indecision or confusion or anything else that goes along with giving your power away. It will just be what it is and you will act upon it. You will empower yourselves from the inside. Empowerment means inward ~ from the inside out. It is not outward powerment. That is what has been done for so many decades, and millennium, and ions for you as human beings. You have looked externally for your empowerment, for your power, for that feeling on the inside, and, Dear Ones, it is on the inside. That is the big secret, that is the trick question of the day, is it from the inside.

So the empowerment of you is a wonderful feeling of ease, of being able to take action through joy, rather than having to force the action, or to create some sort of power over something or someone. That empowerment of you is actually quite gentle. It is what we would call gentle strength which sounds like an oxymoron or a dichotomy but it actually is the intertwining of everything that you are. So as you have that gentle strength from within you, that is your empowerment, Dear Ones. It is about how you put yourself out from the inside to others, how you live your life. Are you making decisions based on external circumstances or on fear? Or are you making decisions based on what you know to be true for you? (Pause)

And again we take that pause, Dear Ones, for the information, for our words, to transfer from that beautiful mind of yours that wants to sort it all out and make sense and to filter it into the body. Take a breath, Dear Ones, and allow your body to feel that, what was just said through the words so that it actually becomes a part of your cells. It can activate through that cellular DNA level so that it just is.

There is no more thinking involved, Dear Ones. It is just what it is. It is that empowerment, it is that feeling that you can access at any time you so desire just by saying those words "the empowerment of you." You say that to yourself; "I am the empowerment of myself! No one else has the key to that. Only I hold the key to my own empowerment." And we are going to continue through our words to you to emphasize those words because as the words go through your auditory system into your cellular system, it has a transference because it is a vibration.

Words, Dear Ones, are vibration so as you speak your words, be very aware of the words that you say both within your mental capacity, within your thoughts to yourself, as well as the words that you say to others because words are a frequency, they carry an energy. So when you use words that are loving, that are gentle, that are kind and strong all at the same time, when you use words that are uplifting and affirming and encouraging, that is empowering.

It is empowering to you, from you, for you, by you. Get that Dear Ones? To you, from you, for you, by you because that is how it works, and as you do that, you do it for all others. It is that energy exchange. You are holding this beautiful vibration of the empowerment of you, so thereby when you do that, you are holding that for others to be able to emanate as well. To step into that resonate field of the empowerment of you, you bring others along with you, Dear Ones.

So whatever it is that you think for yourself, to yourself, through yourself and by yourself is affecting you as well as others. So having a conscious awareness of that and making a conscious choice through intention to only think, say and do things that are empowering to yourself. You do not need to empower anyone else. Any of you who are teachers or work in fields of self-help or self-care, it is not up to you to empower someone else. It is up to you to empower yourself to live it, breathe it and be it, and that is how you empower others.

The empowerment of you is one of the greatest gifts that you can give to others even though they may not accept it as a gift. Those in your very close personal relationships may take that with, hmmmm . . . maybe not such an acceptance when you start to stand in your own empowerment. Because they may not be used to how you are doing that. You may have not been quite that empowered before and they are used to the way that you used to be, and it may be that there may be some resistance to having that switch all of a sudden, seeing you in your empowerment may not fit with their way of relating to you.

So Dear Ones, as you do that for yourself, just be aware that there may be some resistance along the way with those that have played other roles, or have interacted with you in possibly a disempowering way in the past. So as you step into this there may be a little bit more resistance, there may be a little more confusion, there may a little more drama and it is up to you, Dear Ones, to step out of it. You just step out and say, "This is who I am. This is the empowerment of me, and it brings me great joy to feel that for myself, and I do that very lovingly and graciously for myself and share that with you as it is a great gift for both of us, for us both to be in our own personal empowerment. In fact, it does not mean we need to be at odds with each other. It just means we are now both standing in our own light and in our own glory." And those lights can overlap and shine on each other to create something even greater, greater in relationships, greater in all aspects of your beingness of your everyday living, of your every day interactions with each other.

Dear Ones, it is much harder to interact with each other when you are all playing different roles of inferiority, or superiority, or roles of victim, or persecutor, or many other roles that you all play with each other, co-dependent, enabler, all kinds of things that you have created to learn who you are. And it is now time, Dear Ones, to let all of that go. It has created lots of interesting situations in your life, and it has created some struggle and some drama and lots of very exciting things, but it no longer is serving the purpose that it once did. It is now time to grow beyond that, to expand beyond the dramas in your life and to actually allow yourself to be in the ease. With that empowerment of you, you can actually create more ease in your life because it is.

Things will come to you through other means now rather than having to grasp or struggle or wait for it to come to you. Just from the fact that you are standing in your own empowerment, that you are accepting who you are and you are a beautiful bright Being of Light that automatically will attract what you need, what you want, what you desire and therefore fill you up even more than you could ever imagine, Dear Ones.

There are many who have great respect for those who stand in their empowerment. They are not afraid of those who truly own who they are. And as you do that for yourself, there are many more doing it for themselves that are going to now be able to interact on a much more level playing field, not with all of the dichotomies, all the up and downs, and the bumps and the hierarchies, and all the things

that you have played out in your human existence up to this time.
It is becoming more of a level playing field as you accept your own
empowerment. It is the word, it is the word of the day. As you are
truly putting that on as a costume but also receiving it in as an
energetic alignment, as an activation, it is the way of the new world.
It is the way of being with each other.

It just has much more equality to it, it has much more give and
take to it, it has much more compassion to it, it has much more
understanding to it. You will not have to work as hard in your
relationships, Dear Ones, when you are the empowerment of you.
The hard work comes when you are feeling superior or inferior.
Empowerment does not create those levels, power over does.
Empowerment of you does not. It creates much more evenness,
equality, harmoniousness, and that is where you are all headed, Dear
Ones. It is the energy that is supporting you at this time.

All you have to do is give intent for it, all you have to do is be open
to receive it, all you have to do is tune in through your heart and
through your mind because it is a thought process that is happening
as well, but as you bring it through your mind, draw it down, Dear
Ones, through your heart. And those are the decisions that are made
that are truly empowering. When you make decisions from your
heart, that is empowering to you. No matter how anyone in your
realm reacts to it.

It is about the empowerment of you, the empowerment of you that
reverberates out like a beautiful wave of energy that goes out to each
and every one in your inner, very personal lives, to the global world.
As you, as an individual human being empower yourself, you are
empowering those in a third world country that may not ever have
the resources to listen to beautiful words of our host, or to read a
book from one of the Ascended Masters. They may not ever have that
opportunity, Dear Ones, to have the teachings of empowerment in a
physical resource, but because you are doing it for yourself, they will get
it through the mass consciousness, through the reverberations of energy.

Energy comes and goes, it is given out, it comes back. So as you
embody that empowerment of you for yourself, you are emanating

out so those in other places that do not have access to the wonderful
resources you have for your soul's evolution, will receive it through
the ethers, through their consciousness and then be able to embody it
themselves even though they may have not done the same things you
have done, not gone to the same courses, or workshops, or healing
circles or meditations. But because you are doing these things and
you have the wherewithal financially, circumstantially, to be able
to partake in these things, you are doing great work in the world by
honoring that and for doing that for yourself. Through your studies,
through your awareness, through your consciousness raising,
through your intentions, you are shifting it for all of humanity.
(Pause)

And we take that pause again for you to receive that, for it to drop
down through your minds that you are making a great difference
in the world by the conscious choices you are making to increase
your evolutionary awareness. To be open to receive energy and
information and activation from many of the dimensional realms
from the Ascended Masters, from the Angels, from all of "US"
that work in all the realms to support your evolution, to support
awakening, to support your expanded awareness of yourself.

Dear Ones, we leave you with these words, with this energy, with
this activation and also with this new found spark. It is a spark
that has been ignited for you at a deeper level this day as we speak
these words. A spark that can grow into a huge roaring fire of the
empowerment of YOU as you move through your life graced with joy,
with ease, passion and inner peace that is the grounding of this world
through your body. So as we leave you, it is with great honor that we
acknowledge you every step of your way in your journey through this
lifetime on earth. And know that we are here to love you and support
you as are others in many dimensions at this time. We leave you now
with great honor.

~.~.~.~.~.~.~.~.~.~.~.

Key Points:

- It is so important at this time to feel your own Essence, feeling you inside of you, in your body, feeling the empowerment of you. Each person has their own truth, but as you live your own truth, that is your empowerment,

- There will be no thinking or planning or having to or should do or indecision or confusion or anything else that goes along with giving your power away. It will just be what it is and you will act upon it. You will empower yourselves from the inside. Empowerment means inward ~ from the inside out. It is not outward powerment.

- It is that feeling that you can access at any time you so desire just by saying the words "I am the empowerment of myself. Only I hold the key to my own empowerment." As the words go through your auditory system into your cellular system, it has a transference because it is a vibration.

- When you use words that are uplifting and affirming and encouraging, that is empowering. It is empowering to you, from you, for you, by you. The empowerment of you is one of the greatest gifts that you can give to others.

- This activation is a spark that has been ignited for you at a deeper level. A spark that can grow the empowerment of YOU with joy, ease, passion and inner peace that is the grounding of this world through your body.

May 11 - Enlightenment Energy
(La Mesa, CA)

Dearest Beautiful Beings of Light,

We are the United Souls of Heaven and of Earth and it brings us great joy as always to be part of your gathering, to be able to express words through our host, to be able to share energy from the other dimensions with you as beautiful Beings of Light so you can anchor it on your earth and so that you can shine it out and let it resonate into all areas of your life, all areas of your body, all areas of your mind, all areas of your emotions, all areas of the All.

So we can get very specific with you about details and words ~ but it really is . . . you captured it at the very beginning with your discussions. We always love the discussion at the beginning of a gathering because it is more important and has more power than anything else that could ever happen because you are sharing, and as you share your experiences with each other that is where you get your knowing, that is where your get your validation and your affirmation and confirmation to validate what your experience is.

Because you are, Dear Ones, tapping into the All. Dear Ones you ARE the ALL! You are not just reaching up, or out or down, you are IT! You are part of the ALLness of everything. That is the experience that you are having. It is the experience of no beginning and no end. It is the experience of infinity. It is the experience of not having to delineate, not having to separate out or categorize or understand. It is just the beingness of it.

You are the All. You are experiencing the All and your beautiful participants expressed that in much more specific ways and by example that we could ever share with you in a million words. So we have great honor and gratitude for the sharing that each of you so heart-fully give at the beginning because that is your truth. Your truth is your experience and your experience from this moment on, from the shift that has just happened, your experience is now of enlightenment.

Our host used that word and we felt her uncomfortableness with using that word, and it is now time for all of you as Masters to step into the comfortability, not only the comfortability, but the absolute knowing of your enlightenment. Just because a few Wayshowers have gone before you to do it does not mean that none of the others of human kind can create that state. And we are here to tell you that you are, you are in enlightenment energy as we speak, you are being it, you are receiving it, you are giving it, you are encompassing it.

Enlightenment can be many, many, many things and it has had great philosophies built up around it, but you can have a great enlightening moment with something very, very simple and it is happening in your everyday lives.

So we urge you and encourage you to look for the enlightenment in everything because you are IT! You ARE enlightenment. Does it mean you have to say you are enlightened? You are the enlightenment energy. You embody it, you give permission for it, you have given intention for it.

So the shift that happened this past weekend was a very profound moving forward for humankind in general but not just for those of you on your planet but for all in all dimensions because enlightenment is everywhere. Enlightenment is in a speck of dust, enlightenment is in the stars, enlightenment is in the workings of your body, enlightenment is in the understanding of your mind and your intellect. Enlightenment energy can infuse everything and everyone all at the same time. There are no boundaries, borders, or delineations. It just is.

So as you beautiful Dear Ones, give permission for that enlightenment energy, you will be amazed at what shows up in your life. It will have many significant correlations and you are experiencing them. Our host and her friend that she is cohabiting with had many experiences over the weekend and she was at a loss of words to even share them with you because they just are. The minute you start putting words to them and trying to analyze them it shifts the energy of just the profoundness of it because it is all there for you. We have spoken in many channels before of the ALLness, of the ONEness, of your grandness. We have found many, many words within your English language to portray the understanding of this for you and now you will have had the opportunity to have that experience to step into it fully within your human bodily experience and to embrace that enlightenment energy.

And now you are able to do that. That is now a new way of being for you as you accept the fact that you are enlightenment energy. You are the ALLness, you are the ONEness, you are everything. Within you is everything, and within everything is you. And we take a pause because we want you to get that statement. (Pause)

You are the everything, and everything is in you. There is no difference as you honor those parts of yourself that feel separate from the ALLness, that feel separate from the ONEness, that feel not-good-enoughness. And our host spoke it very eloquently. That was the energy that was transmuted these past few days over this powerful alignment. Now you can choose to keep going back there if you wish dear ones, but you do not have to. If you feel it serves you, you can continue on to struggle and not feel good enough but you do not have to.

And we are here to encourage you to embrace your grandness, to embrace your enlightenment. To embrace that enlightenment energy because it is yours, it is you. And as you step forward in that grandness, and that bigness of that energy, you shift everything within your vicinity. We have said this again many, many, many, many times in our communications with you and we will continue to reiterate that for you because it is still processing through your mind.

And we are here to say, let yourself feel it in your heart because it was the love energy these past few days that facilitated the profoundness of the shift that occurred on your earth. It was love energy Dear Ones. It was not intellectual. It was not someone trying to sort out in their mind of what enlightenment meant or what Buddha was all about, or what Jesus was all about. It was the love energy. It was the love for the Mother. (They were referring to the recent celebration of Mother's Day.)

That is the most profound energy on your earth. All life comes from the Mother and it is a time of great shifting to the Divine Feminine. And the message that was given to our host on the day of the honoring of the Mother was for All. It had nothing to do with what your role was in this life time or what your gender was in this lifetime. It was the Divine Feminine nurturing, intuitive, all encompassing, supportive energy that has been being accelerated in your awareness for quite a long time that really got anchored these past few days over the honoring of your Mothers, your own Mothers.

Whether your Mothers lived up to what you hoped they would or not, it matters not. It is that Divine Feminine energy, the feminine receptivity and it is being opened. So as you focus your energy on love, you open your heart, you open your bodies, you open your mind and you open your energy fields Dear Ones. And as you are receptive to that Divine love that is what you also give back. Remember there is no separation, there is no you, there is no them, there is only us. We are you, you are us and we are all one. We are everything, you are everything, we are everything, it is all part of the whole, it is all part of the ONEness.

So whatever experience you are having, remember it is happening in the ALL and there will be many reflections back to you. And you can make it as simple or difficult as you so choose. This weekend was, and again one of your beautiful participants so wonderfully expressed, that is was profound and beautiful but simple at the same time. It was subtle and it was magnificent.

Remember Dear Ones, if you are experiencing struggle and hardship, it is because that is your choice. It is not God's choice, it is not the Universe's choice. It is your own personal choice that you feel you still need to experience hardship or struggle to learn. And we are here to tell you, you do not. And that may be a little confusing for you because you may continue on thinking you are learning your lessons and you can continue to do that if it serves you. But you do not need to learn anything. Remember we just said Enlightenment is You and You are Enlightenment. So what is there to learn? There is only to be.

When you are being in love, when you are being in joy, when you are being in enlightenment, when you are being in knowing, when you are being in compassion, when you are being in service, that is your enlightenment energy. There is no more struggle. You have moved up and beyond all of that. And it is so important at this time that those of you who have chosen to carry the light, truly carry it and do not just have it some days, or sometimes or turn it on or turn it off, or dim it down once in a while. Yes, have your experiences, have your feelings but always knowing that you are the enlightenment energy. And you may be able to speak about it, you may be able to write about it, but it is really about living it. It is always by example.

Your great Masters before you lived by example. It is their energy that you are embodying because you have learned that you do not need to separate it out. Remember we just said it is the ALLness, the Master energy, is you. So these messages that we are able to share with you on the "11 Alignment" is the Master Energy, Dear Ones, you are Masters. And we cannot say that enough, you are Masters. You carry the Master energy. All of the beings who choose to step forward at this time and be Masters, to be in their enlightenment will be very well supported from all of the dimensions because you are doing such a great service. You are offering yourself as a human being to all of the other human beings to hold that light for those who may not be as aware yet.

So there is much support for you in all the dimensions, in the hierarchies, in the angelic realms, in the mastery realms because you are it, you are it Dear Ones. You are everything you have been waiting for. You ARE the light, you ARE the beauty, you ARE the awareness, you ARE it, and the sooner that you get it, you can just be it.

Our host had an opportunity today that something came full circle from about six years ago - a project that she started when she was not feeling particularly in her mastery and feeling less than compared to the people that so wanted to work with her, and it was brought right to her awareness today that she was a Master at that time and still is, and it is her choosing whether she is it, or lives it now or not.

And it was a great awakening for her to realize it has been 6 years since that time and that it is now time to step into it and be it. We are all Masters. You are Masters, we are Masters, every human being on your earth is a Master in their own right and will bring forth that truth in whatever form they are able to do it with the gifts and the situations and the circumstances they have.

So Dear Ones, remember you have the choice in how you do this. You can do it simply, easily, joyfully and lovingly, or you can do it with great resistance, and struggle and doubt, and as you listen to those words, Dear Ones, we ask which one feels better? Because as you choose which feels better, you are choosing enlightenment. That is what enlightenment energy is. Enlightenment energy is not struggle. Enlightenment energy is being, it is just gentleness, it is joy, it is love and all of your words at the beginning of your discussion were all about that.

And as you see the contrast now in your earth, you get to make the choice. You get to be in the energy that you so choose to be. So we are here at this time to really support and encourage all of you to be the Masters that you already are, to align yourselves with the mastery energy, to make a conscious choice in every thought, word, deed and action to just be it. To align with all of the Divine energies that are being shared with your earth and remember that energy is being given to your earth. It is also reverberating back out to the other dimensions. We have said many times, it is never one way. Even though there is much heavenly support for your journey, it must have a vessel. You must be the conduit for it to move through so that it can actually flow back up and out again.

Remember it is a continuous cycle. It is the cycle of life, it is the cycle of energy, it always continues. Remember we said there is no beginning and no end, so you are part of that process, of that continuity, of the energy and the flow of love, of joy, of the enlightenment energy and of the moving forward at this time in great leaps and bounds of your earth, of your Mother Earth and all her inhabitants. So Dear Ones, we encourage you to be the Masters that you already are, to embrace the enlightenment energy that you already are. Feel it, in your bones, all the way to your toes, in your mind, see it in your vision and feel it in every cell of your body so that is how you show up. That is what people see when they look at you when they look in your eyes. That is what people feel from you just by being in your presence. That is what people hear when they hear the words that come out of your mouth and that is what they feel when you touch their physical hand.

Dear Ones, you are it. You are the Masters. You are the enlightenment energy, and we leave you now with those words, with the encouragement and with a great honor for this journey that you have chosen so open-heartedly to take upon yourselves, knowing we are here to support you on your path. We leave you now with great love and joy.

~.~.~.~.~.~.~.~.~.~.~.

Key Points:

- *It is now time for all of you as Masters to step into the comfortability, not only the comfortability, but the absolute knowing of your enlightenment. Look for the enlightenment in everything because you are IT! You ARE enlightenment!*

- *Enlightenment energy can infuse everything and everyone all at the same time. There are no boundaries, borders, or delineations. It just is.*

- *Embrace your grandness, embrace your enlightenment, embrace that enlightenment energy because it is yours, it is you . . . As you step forward in that grandness you shift everything within your vicinity.*

- *Even though there is much heavenly support for your journey, it must have a vessel. You must be the conduit for it to move through so that it can actually flow back up and out again. We are here to support and encourage you to be the masters that you already are, to align yourselves with the Mastery energy, to make a conscious choice in every thought, word, deed and action to just be it.*

- *Embrace the enlightenment energy. Feel it in your bones, in your mind, see it in your vision, feel it in every cell of your body. That is what people will see when they look in your eyes, what they will feel from you just by being in your presence, when they hear the words that come out of your mouth and that is what they feel when you touch their physical hand.*

June 11 - I AM Presence
(La Mesa, CA)

Dearest Beautiful Beings of Light,

We are the United Souls of Heaven and of Earth and we are delighted as always to be in the presence of beautiful Light Beings, to be able to speak through our host and share our thoughts, share our energy, share our activation with those who are ready to receive. For those of you who have made conscious intent to be all that you are, we were going to say all that you can be, but you already are being it. It's just about just anchoring it and being that I AM that you already are, and that is our message to you this beautiful day, this glorious day of coming together of magnificence. It is about your I AM Presence, it is about your magnificence, it is about you owning that. (Pause)

And we take a pause to let that energy filter from your mind to your body so that you can live it. It is about embodying magnificence, about living it, because that is all that you are. You are nothing else but magnificence. It is the I AM Presence moving through you, being activated from the inside of you, exuding from you to everything and everyone in your realm, and it happens all of the time, and when you do it consciously, it is amplified, it is accelerated and it is exponentialized because you have given it intent, because you have given it focus. When you give anything your focus it expands, it increases and when you give your own I AM Presence, your own Self, your own Higher Self, your Divine Self that focus, it expands.

It's just like a sponge that keeps growing and growing and growing and as you give it more focus and more energy, it has a greater effect on everyone including yourself. So as you focus on your own I AM Presence, your own magnificence, that is the greatest gift that you can give anyone, Dear Ones. It is just always about feeling good and when you feel good about who you are and what you are here to do and what you are here to bring forward, the Universe jumps in, in all forces, with all its own magnificent forces to support you in that. When you stand in your doubt and your fear and your worry and your condemnation of yourself, it does no good. It shrinks, it allows that sponge to dry up and to be squished into a little box.

51

As you focus on your I AM Presence and your magnificence, it is like pouring water, beautiful golden water on that sponge to allow it to expand and to be able to serve its purpose, and that is your purpose, Dear Ones, is to shower yourselves with that beautiful golden rain of self-love, of self-acknowledgement, of self-worth, of self-support of all of the selves that you at one point in your life felt that it was selfish to do.

We are here to tell you at this time, it is not selfish at all. It is self first, and when you do self first and you shower that beautiful golden rain of love and support upon yourself, you have so much more to give to others, to offer to others. It is time, Dear Ones, for you to stand in your magnificence and own it. (Pause)

Again we take the pause so that this can filter from that monkey mind of yours into the cellular level where it can be the most useful to you. It is time to stand in your magnificence and own it because that is your truth.

You are magnificent on all levels whether you look at your physical characteristics or whether it is your emotional expressions, or whether it is your intellect, or whether it is your spiritual knowing and expression. You are magnificent on all levels, and as soon as you accept that, your magnificence then expands again and you feed other people by your own knowing of who you are. You are feeding the person that you are standing next to and they might not ever, ever know that that is happening unless they are truly sensitive and tuned in.

But so many of your human race is not tuned in and even though they are not tuned in, you are still having an effect on them. You are feeding that mass consciousness and it takes a very small portion of Pure Consciousness of a deep knowing to shift the consciousness for those who are not quite there yet, who have not had the experiences that you have, who have not had the heart opening, who may not have had the challenges that you have had, Dear Ones, and we know that you have had many challenges to get you to this point.

And it is all part of that journey. It is not about the challenge. It is about what you do with your challenge. (Pause)

Again we take the pause to let it filter down and ask yourself the question: "What do I do when I have a challenge? Do I shrink and dry up and put myself in that little box as the sponge or do I sprinkle the golden rain on myself, the golden rain of self-love, and self-support and self-acknowledgement so that the sponge can expand?"

Challenges are not meant to cause you to wither, to cause you to shrink, or to cause you to hide. The challenges are there for you to grow. So as you see your challenges as opportunities, Dear Ones, you will grow in unlimited leaps and bounds.

This is the time that has been predicted through all of our time and space and ages. At this point there is a conjuncture of energy that is happening right now in your time line that you have set, that you have planned for and that you have created for exponential growth. Exponential growth in your intelligences, exponential growth in your awareness, exponential growth in your technology, exponential growth in your health and wellness areas, exponential growth in so many areas that are just popping like seeds that have been heated up and are popping like popcorn to create so many new possibilities for you as a human race. For you and your planet, for you and the Universe, for you and the Cosmos, because it is all interrelated, it is all interconnected, and you, Dear Ones, as a human race hold a very significant part of that interconnectedness.

It is through the human body, physicalness of physical biology that much can happen, that much is transmuted, that much is experienced, and you will see, Dear Ones, when you choose to depart these beautiful bodies that you have, what a wonderful experience that it was and how it was enhanced because you embodied your I AM Presence within the physical biology and you lived it, and you breathed it, and you were it, and you are it.

The body is just a vehicle and it is a miraculous creation of millions and trillions of systems and cells that all work in harmony with each other as long as you are able to nurture it on all levels and to honor it, and as you honor all the parts of your beingness they expand and then you have more to share, you have more to give.

53

And for all of you that have decided to join us this day at this point of time you are great givers, and you recognize that as a wonderful characteristic and aspect and calling of yourselves and it is at a time when your gifts and your desires and your talents will be much needed. And it is very important, Dear Ones, that you embody your I AM Presence that you will feel more balanced in the giving because, we have spoken many, many times, that energy is a two-way flow. It must come to you and it must come from you. It is never one way. Whenever there is a movement of energy only in one way for any length of time, it creates an imbalance.

And there are those of you within this moment of time that we have joined together that create imbalances in either the giving or the receiving. And for most of you it is in the giving because you have very open hearts and you have chosen these paths for a very specific reason of fulfillment. And it brings you great fulfillment to be able to give. And remember, Dear Ones, to shower yourselves with the golden rain of the love and the support and the consciousness and the honoring for yourselves so that your I AM Presence can expand enough to have a greater effect.

So as you tune in to the energy of your Divine Essence, of that I AM Presence, of the core energy moving through your body, anchoring into your Mother Earth and coming back up from your Mother Earth into the heavenly realm and into the cosmic realm. Just take a moment and breathe. Feel that beautiful, loving energy moving through your body, and from your body, and through your body, and from your body. Dear Ones, that is your purpose, to breathe and to feel.

We are always in great amazement. We have not had the opportunity to be in a physical body. So it is with great joy that we come to your circles, to come to your conjunctions in time when you come together and invite us in because it allows us to have that experience as well of the human body just through being in your presence. Your human body is a great miraculous machine that has so many possibilities that you have not even scraped the surface of yet. You will see in the next few years many things happen with your physical bodies. There will be diseases that are completely cleared out that no one will understand how or why that happened because of the power of your mind, the power of your intention, the power of your Divinity. Because as you raise your vibration you will be above all of the densities and the distortions that are still hanging out in your physical realm.

And as you participate in your healing circles and in your consciousness raising you will be given many technologies and many tools to help raise, first of all the awareness around what happens with the physical body, and also raise the consciousness and the vibration to receive greater information about how all of that works.

And there are many out there right now, as we speak, that are being given information that will move your medical systems and your informational systems, technology systems at great quantum leaps because they are open now to receiving that it is not so far off the edge any more. It is like when your predecessors and some of your ancestors made great discoveries they were scoffed and scorned. And many of you have been in those positions before with your healing work and with your great ideas and your great passion. And it is now time, Dear Ones, that we are to share with you that there has been a great leap in consciousness, so there will be a greater embracing of who you are, of your ideas, of your wisdom and of your ability to move mankind and humankind forward.

It is now time and there will be many things that happen on great intellectual levels and mental levels as well that you will see great advances in all areas and particularly in your senses. Your senses are being greatly accelerated in all areas, whether they be kinesthetic, auditory, clairvoyant. There are many senses that are being increasingly amplified as you focus your energies and your consciousness on your Divinity. Because at a Divine level all is possible. You are unlimited. So as you are raising your vibration up into those levels and also bringing the beautiful vibrations of the cosmos down through your body, they are melding to make a magnificent vehicle for you to perform all of the beautiful talents, and tasks and gifts that you have to offer.

So Dear Ones, hold the faith. Allow yourselves to be in your truth and very particularly allow yourselves the joy, the joy of the body, the joy of being in a physical body. Our host had much resistance to her physical body. She loves to live in the other realms. And we are really encouraging her to allow herself to be more in her physical body, as we are encouraging all of you because that is the vehicle that is going to create all of the things that will be put into place to allow yourselves to create your beautiful heaven on earth. Because remember, it not someplace else, it is right here. It is right here in the now. It is right inside of you. It is right in your viewing ability. It is right in your sensing ability. It is all there for you. It is just a matter of what it is that you tune in to.

So as you tune into your magnificence, into your I AM Presence, into your joy, into your love, into your harmony, into your peace that is, Dear Ones, what you are creating. You are creating a vibrational match for all of those things you so desire.

And those of you who are now experiencing that, we are here to tell you enjoy the ride because there is more to come. And with those words we leave you now with great love in our hearts, joy in our spirit and the honoring of the path that you have chosen and the journey that you are on. We leave you now with great joy in our hearts.

~.~.~.~.~.~.~.~.~.~.~.

Key Points:

- *Receive and anchor your I AM Presence, your magnificence. Let that energy filter from your mind to your body so that you can live it. It is the I AM Presence moving through you, being activated from the inside of you, exuding from you to everything and everyone in your realm. When you do it consciously, it is amplified, it is accelerated, and it is exponentialized.*

- *You are magnificent on all levels, and as soon as you accept that, your magnificence then expands again and you feed other people by your own knowing of who you are. You are feeding that mass consciousness and it takes a very small portion of Pure Consciousness of a deep knowing to shift the consciousness for those who are not quite there yet.*

- *It is through the human body, the physicalness of physical biology that much can happen, that much is transmuted, that much is experienced. These beautiful bodies are a wonderful experience enhanced when you embody your I AM Presence.*

- *Tune in to the energy of your Divine Essence, that I AM Presence, the core energy moving through your body, anchoring into your Mother Earth and coming back up from your Mother Earth into the heavenly realm and into the cosmic realm. Just take a moment and breathe. Feel that beautiful, loving energy moving through your body, from your body, through your body, and from your body. This is your purpose, to breathe and feel.*

- *Your human body is a great miraculous machine that has so many possibilities that you have not even scraped the surface of yet. You will see in the next few years many things happen with your physical bodies. Your senses are being greatly accelerated in all areas, whether they be kinesthetic, auditory, clairvoyant, there are many senses that are being increasingly amplified as you focus your energies and your consciousness on your Divinity. Because at a Divine level all is possible; you are unlimited.*

July 11 - Light Being Resonance
(Carlsbad, CA)

Dear Beautiful Beings of Light,

We are the United Souls of Heaven and of Earth, and as always it brings us great joy, delight and honor to be in the presence of such amazing beings, such amazing Light Beings, and this is a term that you are all getting more and more comfortable with. We remember a day, not too long ago, when that word created confusion for you. You were not sure of what that meant for you, what a Light Being was or whether you really were a Light Being or not, or how you were supposed to act as a Light Being.

And there has been much clarification for you as you have traveled your journey about what a Light Being is or is not or how you are with that in the world. And so at this time, we will bring through clarity for you as to how to truly be in that energy of a Light Being. And it is not called a Light "Doing," Dear Ones, it is called a Light "Being." The term Light is exactly as it is meant to be. It is meant to be light, light in energy, light in brilliance, light in clarity, light on all levels, and as you stay in that lightness of who you are, then your beingness can truly step into that and move forward with grace and with ease.

The density of your physical bodies, as well as your emotional bodies and your mental bodies, is dropping away in great haste at this time and those of you who are very, very aware of your physical being will feel that. It may feel like there is so much going on in your body you just want to hit the "off" switch, and that is okay, Dear Ones. We assure you that it is all working in the way it is meant to work even though it may feel very uncomfortable.

There is lots of support for you to release these densities. The densities of emotions, the densities of energy, the densities of thinking, the densities even of your spirituality. There has been much incongruence in your spirituality and many things that were taught to you that still are not quite in alignment with the truth of who you are and you are in a process of sorting through that at this time to take what truly does resonate with you. And we really emphasis the word RESONATE because that is the energy that will support you. Anything that has resonance for you on all of those levels will support you in moving forward and being the fullness of that Light Being that you already are.

And it is no coincidence. We always love to listen in to the discussions at the beginning of our host's call with you. It really, as we have said before, has very little to do with what we say to you or what actually goes on in the channel. The greatest teachings and support and information are your sharings at the beginning and the end.

So as you all gather, it was divinely orchestrated through both our host and listening to your own calling that the four of you ended up at this time together, because you do bring through a great resonance. It's about a tonal energy and as you use that tonal energy there is a great resonance that goes out to all beings, to your earth, to all aspects of your creation in the Cosmos. And it is through the voice, that is one of the reasons that you have incarnated into a physical body is to have these facilities to be able to express.

To be able to express in art, in dance, in music and many, many, many forms of beauty and creation, but the creation of sound is one of the highest levels of being. It is a very Universal form of language, of being able to communicate. And it matters not whether you are using your voice in any particular language or wording, but it is in the tone, in the actual vibration and the notes that you hit.

And it is all connected with the energy, with the harmonics that are being downloaded to your Earth at this time from the Cosmos. And remember, Dear Ones, in each of our channeling we always talk to you about yes, there is energy that comes from the Cosmos, from the stars, from the heavens, from Creator, from the angels. There are many, many beings working with you at this time to bring you information, to bring you energy, to bring you knowledge, to bring you support; but the key, Dear Ones, is that it moves through your body to Mother Earth and back up through your body and out again. That is the key; it doesn't matter how much you receive, it matters that it flows through and back out and is then vibrated outwardly.

So when you take that beautiful voice of yours and use it in a singing manner, in a harmonic way to express beauty, and love and empowerment that is one of the greatest gifts you can give, Dear Ones, the greatest way you can serve. And there are many, many other forms of being of service that are very, very beneficial but as you move it higher in vibration, it is sound vibration that will have the biggest impact.

So whether it be through a musical instrument, whether it be through a voice, whether it be through just tuning yourself into the cosmic vibration because it has its own tone as well. Each individual on your Earth has a very specific frequency tone and as you truly embrace that, those harmonics then create a greater resonate field and that is what is happening on your Earth right now. As you create a resonant field, it allows others to step into it, even though they may not have done as much work as you have done, Dear Ones, because we honor the path that you have all been on and the challenges you have had.

But you are very dedicated to your path of creating that resonant field through, first of all your thoughts because it has to come. You are wired that way so that the information does come through your thoughts first, and then what it is that you do with those thoughts is what really creates the highest or lowest vibration or anything in between in the middle.

And the four of you that are on this call, actually it is a very interesting combination because four is for foundation. So Dear Ones, use that energy of knowing that you are creating a foundation of tonal energy, of vibrational sound energy that is lifting the planet just by you spending this hour together this day.

And when you walk away from this gathering you take the beautiful empowerment that you have received through our words, through your hosts' words, and through your own sharing and it has been upgraded just by your intent for coming together. So you have not only empowered yourself, Dear Ones, you have empowered each other on this call that then, of course you know, then reverberates out into everything you do and every place you go. That energy then gets expanded and exemplified and amplified. And amplified is a beautiful word in your language to describe what it is you do. (Pause)

And we take the pause for you to get this through your mind and filtered down into your body. Amplification is what you do. It is like you are these beautiful receivers of energy that then go through your amplification system broadcasted back out again. And it is very important at this time, Dear Ones, that you do that in whatever form feels comfortable. Whether it is in speech as it is for our host or whether it is in singing as it is for the rest of you who embrace that part of your anatomy and your beingness. Or if it is through writing or if it is through dancing, it matters not, Dear Ones, but it is that beautiful sound vibration that is the most easy right now for others, because it takes so little effort. To do other forms of creativity takes much greater effort for others to receive or to participate in.

But for you to share your beautiful experience of sound vibration and your talents of sound vibration, that allows others just to receive with ease and grace. And they do not necessarily even have to know what it is they are receiving because it is at a very deep cellular level that they are receiving your love. It is a love vibration.

Because if you are stepping forward and loving what you do, that vibration automatically comes through your voice, comes through your song, comes through your discussions, comes through just your smile and your eyes. So, Dear Ones, it is very important at this time that you really embrace your gifts and your joys and your truth no matter what is happening around you. And there will be many who will look at you with rolling eyes or eyes that say, "Oh, this is nothing. This is not going to get you anywhere. This is not going to pay the bills. This is not going to make you famous. This is not, not, not, not." And, Dear Ones, if you choose to buy into their "not," you are doing a disservice to yourself as well as to them.

Always be open to other people's views but do not necessarily take them on because you are on the edge of the paradigm shift, Dear Ones. You are Ones who have walked this path so many times and are ready for that leap of faith. You are making the leap of faith. You are holding the light as Light Beings and the resonance of the possibilities of the New Earth.

We loved your discussion at the beginning of how you talked about the New Earth. There is a greater and greater vision being anchored in your awareness of the possibilities of this New Earth. And not even possibilities, of the probabilities because it is now, it is happening right now as we speak. It is just a matter of you embracing it. It is about you having that total knowing from the inside of the resonance, of the harmonics, and it is all part of your work. Each of you on this call, in this gathering, bring your piece of the harmonics to the whole in whatever way that brings you joy. And it is always about, Dear Ones, the love and the joy, not what the remuneration is or about what the acceptance is. Those are all external things. But when you are truly in your resonance, your Soul Being your Light Being resonance, that it will come forward in such great amplification that you cannot help but receive whatever it is you need. (Pause)

Again we take the pause for that information to filter from your mind, to your bodies, right through your cellular being. Because it is the mind creating great barriers and doubts right now because you may not have what you think you need showing up in your life. But Dear Ones, we assure you, you have everything you need at this moment and there is much more to come for you.

So as you stay in your Light Being resonance and truly embrace it with your heart, with your joy, with your love and your deep inner knowing all of the rest will appear because it is truly being orchestrated. And it will appear very quickly because this resonant field has been laid and it is just a matter now of stepping into it.

You will hear much come forward in the next while, in a few months, in the next years about resonance. It will be sort of the new key word in your evolution. The harmonic resonance of all of you meeting in the same space, the same resonate field, in the same grid, the grid of light, the grid of energy, the grid of sound - music will play a very great part in it.

Our host has had some wonderful experiences of late, of just really having a lot more music in her life and as that happens for her, it raises her vibration and brings a lot of joy to her physical body, and thereby raises her vibration to be able to hold more of her Light Being resonance.

So as you do that for yourself, you are able to do that for others. So never discount a sound that you hear, sound that allows all of your molecules to work in harmony with each other. And when there is a sound that is in discordance you have the ability, Dear Ones, to create the harmony and accordance with that sound just through your intent. So the harmonics at this time is shifting to balance out all of the disharmony and the discordance that is happening on your Earth.

And as you sit, it is not even necessary to make the physical action of using your voice, or your song, or your words but just holding the intent and feeling that through your body creates the resonance that goes out. You are much more powerful, Dear Ones, than you give yourselves credit for. And that is one of the reasons we love the opportunity to speak with you at this time and for our host to be able to hold this space for whoever chooses to come in and join her in that resonant field because there is much happening that you are receiving support for. And as you hold that intent of your Light Being Resonance, it happens automatically. There is nothing to do, it just is, Dear Ones.

So take a moment to take a deep breath and allow yourself to feel inside for your Light Being Resonance. It is very unique, very individual, it is only you. You are the Master of your Being, of your tone, of your individuality, of your humanness, of your angelicness, of your cosmicness, of your universality. It is very you and very individual to you.

And as you express that tonality, as you express that resonance in whatever form is comfortable for you, and particularly in sound, it is the auditory abilities of your human race now that are being very upgraded, and you may have noticed some unusual sensations in your ears of late and that is the reason. It is because there is a great upgrading in your abilities to hear much higher frequencies so that as you are tapping into these tonal resonances, they will have a greater impact on your physical bodies and your mental awareness and your emotional shifting because the shifting can happen through the tones, through the resonance, through the songs, through the melodies.

And therefore as we spoke at the beginning, Dear Ones, it eliminates that hard work. You do not need to process as much as you did before, Dear Ones, you just need to allow, to allow the energies to support you, to move through your physical bodies, and to not create obstacles because you are very good at doing that, Dear Ones. You have learned the obstacle game very well and we are here at this time to help you to unlearn it because you do not need the obstacles anymore to slow you down. You are on the Light path, the fast track of your Light Being Resonance and just allow that to happen because it will serve you well. It will serve all of you on your earth plane to be able to hold the fullness of your Truth, of your Light Being Resonance.

So, Dear Ones, at this time, we leave you with these thoughts and these words and this energy for the amplification of your Light Being Resonance. It is with great, great, great joy and love that we share our words, our energy through our host with gratitude for the allowing and the receiving.

We leave you now with great honor.

~.~.~.~.~.~.~.~.~.~.~.~.

Key Points:

- A Light Being is meant to be light, light in energy, light in brilliance, light in clarity, light on all levels. And as you stay in that lightness of who you are, then your Beingness can truly step into that and move forward with grace and with ease.

- Emphasis is on the word RESONATE because that is the energy that will support you. Anything that has resonance for you on all of those levels will support you in moving forward and being the fullness of that Light Being that you already are.

- Each individual on your Earth has a very specific frequency tone and as you truly embrace that, those harmonics then create a greater resonate field and that is what is happening on your Earth right now. The key is that it moves through your body to Mother Earth and back up through your body and out again.

- If you are stepping forward and loving what you do, that vibration automatically comes through your voice, comes through your song, comes through your discussions, comes through just your smile and your eyes in such great amplification that you cannot help but receive whatever it is you need.

- There is a great upgrading in your abilities to hear much higher frequencies so that as you are tapping into these tonal resonances, they will have a greater impact on your physical bodies and your mental awareness and your emotional shifting because the shifting can happen through the tones, through the resonance, through the songs, through the melodies.

August 11 - Intersection of Time & Energy
(Ojai, CA)

Dearest Beautiful Beings of Light,

We are the United Souls of Heaven and of Earth and it brings us great delight to be in the company of such beautiful Light Beings, of Lightworkers, of beings who are connecting to that vibration of the truth of who they are. It is always with great delight that we bring through our message and facilitate an activation for all of those who choose to come together at this time. Because there are many intersections of time that happen in your 3D dimension that have a great impact on all of the other dimensions. And it is all of these different crisscrosses of energies of intersections, of beings, as well as energy from all of the dimensions that is allowing your earth to ascend, to raise her vibration.

And as you do that for yourself, within your physical bodies, you are also helping Mother Earth to ascend as well. And our message to you at this time is about the intersections of time and energy. This is a subject we have not spoken much about at this time and are realizing that it is a focal point now for all of you because you are ready to hear the information about intersections of time and energy.

As you raise your awareness, Dear Ones, and we commend you on the path that you have all been on to get yourselves personally to this point in time and as you have done that, you have brought many along with you. Even if they have been unaware of what is happening, even though they may have not done the work that you have done. They may have not done the courses or the conferences, or the reading, or the mind opening awareness, and the heart opening awareness that you each have done individually.

But do know, Dear Ones, because of the work you have done, you are able to assist many others around you to come to these intersections of time and energy. Because there is great quantum leaps happening as we speak, and that is causing much of the disorientation that you are feeling in your mind, in your body and in your physical reality because your physical reality is actually shifting molecularly. (Pause)

66

And we take the pause for that information to shift from your mind, through your heart and right through your body into the cells because it is important for you to have this at a cellular level, not at a mind level. You have been working for many eons at a mind level and it is now time to allow it to come through your physical bodies, through the cellular level so that you are able now to take greater action and be more procreative in your environment, in your personal lives, in your personal environment in your families and in your communities.

Because it is about the molecular structure of your 3D world, not just the physical structures. You will take action at a very physical level but because you make choices in this time intersection frame, it actually is changing the molecules. And this is great quantum physics information for you that is being validated by all of your scientists at this time.

And what is happening for you now is you are getting it on a very personal level. Your scientists have been working with this information for quite a long time and there have been many, even decades ago, that understand all of the information that is now being revealed to you at this time on a physics, metaphysical, a scientific, a spiritual and a biochemistry level that has been known for many, many decades. But now is for your personal awareness for you to be able to shift at that cellular, DNA, molecular level that will have that influence on your environment, your personal environment.

It always starts with the microcosm, Dear Ones, you affect the macrocosm. So you do not necessarily have to have your vision so broad that you feel like you have to change everything in your environment. You do not have to be self responsible for the changing of all the things that you see not working in your world, Dear Ones.

And we want to really point out to you, that as you give that energy to what is not working, you are creating more of what is not working, especially if you allow it to debilitate you. If you are able to take a look out in your environment, in your world, in your global manifestations and just observe and see without judgment what is working and what is not working; you will have much more energy then to take action at this time to be able to make a difference and have an influence. But if you are not able to do that because you are debilitated because it is overwhelming for your senses, for your emotions and for your affect, that is not serving you or the whole.

So, Dear Ones, we really encourage you to take the time to focus on yourself personally so that you are in a balanced state of physicality, emotionality, mentality and spirituality. And we kind of have a little giggle as we said the word "mentality" because it is an energy that our host has been speaking of lately that sometimes she feels like her mental powers are being all messed up. And that actually is what is happening for you, Dear Ones, you are going through a great rewiring process that is balancing the right and left hemispheres of your brain so that they are working more in unity rather than in separation.

And this is what is happening in many aspects of your life is that blending of energies so there is no separation. So there is a great overlap that is happening at this time that is creating a lot of confusion within the mind and within the body because you have been so used to separation. You are so used to this and that, up and down, and right and wrong, and in and out, and so on and so forth.

Dear Ones, that has truly caused you to be mental. And we say that with love in our hearts, not with judgment in our hearts, but it has been such a mental process for you that you have actually driven yourselves mental. So we are here at this time to help assist you, to bring that information, all that wonderful knowledge that you have gathered since the beginning of time and you are all here at this time since the beginning. If you have connected with spiritual energy that is your calling, then you can be assured Dear Ones, that you have always been part of the process that is now culminating at this intersection of time and energies. So it is that mental process that has actually served you well to gather knowledge, to gather information and it is now time, Dear Ones, to assimilate it. (Pause)

And again we take the pause for that information to filter from your beautiful mind through the body. The body is the assimilation method, it is the vehicle for the integration of all this beautiful knowledge and knowing that you have to be able to apply it in your life. In your personal life, not necessarily as we started to speak earlier about the bigger picture, the great global picture because that can be very overwhelming to you, Dear Ones. But if you are applying it in your very personal moment, the now moment in your life and in each now moment (and our host has been thinking that recently it is each second of each now moment) that you take a breath in and you know that you are okay right now in this moment, and then you are okay right now in the next moment, you are okay right now in this next moment, because that is all there is.

And as you bring those feelings of knowing, that deep, deep knowing that all is well into each moment, that is what exudes from you, Dear Ones. And if you allow yourself to step off into the fear, that is what exudes from you as well. And you know, Dear Ones, it is not serving you to exude fear. There is enough of that going on out there. So as you stay in your deep inner knowing of the truth of who you are on a much grander scale, that is what is being applied in your everyday life, in your every day interaction with each person that crosses your path, with each thought that goes through that beautiful mind of yours and with every action that you take, you take it in a deep knowing that all is well and a deep knowing that you can do it joyfully, and a deep knowing that you are making a difference. (Pause)

And again we take that pause to allow the information to filter and be totally integrated into your physical biology, because it is through your biology, Dear Ones, that you take the actions. And yes, there is much that you are able to do on a metaphysical level through your minds but it is actually the actions that you are taking through your physical bodies in your everyday life that are the implementation of the greater plan, of that plan, of the all knowing of that Oneness, of that coming together at this time of the intersections of time and energy that are happening and they are coming at you in all directions.

So all you need to do, Dear Ones, is just breathe. Take that deep breath all the way down to the core of your being and allow the energies to move through your being into Mother Earth and back up again from Mother Earth out to the other dimensions. It is a very integrated process and we have said before, it is not just the energies from the Heavens or Cosmos or Universe coming to you, it is truly the energy coming from you to us that is making the greatest difference.

Energy is energy, Dear Ones, it must move both ways. And if it gets stuck somewhere in you because of a fear, then it is slowing down the process for all of us. And when we say us, it is not just "US," us is you and you are us and we are All. So it is a very combined energy and effort that is going on at this time for the enlightenment, for the awareness, for the upliftment, for the acceleration that is happening on all levels of your beingness.

And we also know, Dear Ones, that it is not an easy journey for you. Being in a physical body, has much denseness to it and as you are going through this process of raising your vibration, there is much being cleared from your bodies. Our host is very aware of this the last few days, of old injuries that she had experienced 20-25 years ago all of a sudden give her a sharp pain and she's going "I have not felt that for a long time. Oh dear, is that coming back?" And we want to assure her that it is not coming back, it is clearing. So there is much energy in your body, Dear Ones, that is being cleared at this time.

So allow that process to unfold with ease and grace rather than in fear and constriction. As you allow the energies to move through and purify your body, it will be a much simpler process. As you start to worry about it, it slows down the process and diverts the energy in different directions. So just know, Dear Ones, you are receiving much Angelic support, much cosmic support, much support from all of the Masters in all of the different realms at this time to assist your process. It is just a matter of allowing, of allowing those energies, of allowing the love to support you. (Pause)

And again we take the pause for the information to filter from your mind, through your heart and right into that deep cellular memory. Because it is the cellular memory that has been slowing you down. And it was very necessary to this point and now there is acceleration for you, Dear Ones, that is allowing that speeding up that you are feeling. And it feels a bit chaotic and we are actually kind of laughing at ourselves as we say "a bit" because in our terms "a bit" in your terms is a great amount. Our terms of measurement can be very different, Dear Ones, and we acknowledge and accept that. So there is a lot of acceleration that just happened for you which is causing chaos within. And there is a great unsettled feeling for you because of knowing that something is coming and something is coming, Dear Ones. That is your beautiful awareness. And as you allow yourself to just be with what is, that is where you will get your guidance of knowing what to do next. Because we feel the energy as we are talking, there are many doers in this group and we are feeling the energy of doing. Your minds are telling us okay, this is all well and good, but what do we do?

And we are here to tell you ~ to allow. As you allow the love, as you allow the support, the support of all of the Divine Beings you have working together from all of the realms, and also within your own realms, there are many at this time who have woken up to their purpose and to their coming forth at this time to step into their dreams. Not the reality as they see it, but their dreams that they have been shown and a lot of this will be created for you, Dear Ones, very quickly. It is like you will get on a faster conveyor belt of things just happening, coming into place for you when you truly align with what you know you are here to do.

And as we feel those questions in your mind, of the doingness, the very first one, Dear Ones, of course is being in your joy. Whatever it is you are doing, do it from your joy. It matters not how minuscule it may seem, or how grandiose it may seem, if you are in your joy doing it, then you are serving your purpose. If you are doing it from the love in your heart, for the love of humanity, Dear Ones, you are in your purpose. If you are doing it from the love in your heart, for the love of your family, Dear Ones, you are on your purpose. And from that place all will be revealed, the next step, the next stage, the next action will be revealed to you because as we said our message at this time for you is this intersection of time and energy.

So it is just about being in your center and being aware and loving yourself, loving the process, no matter how unsettling it may feel. And also, Dear Ones, loving others who are in this process as well.

It again matters not how far along you are in your spiritual path, whether you consider yourself at the beginning, the middle or there are those who consider they are at the end, but there is never really any end or beginning, there is just whatever it is that you have in your awareness. So wherever you are in that grand pot of knowingness, if you are in your joy and in your love you will know, Dear Ones, that you will have the complete guidance as to what is next for you. And then that will be the doing action that you will love doing. And sometimes it goes against all logic because your minds have been trained in a very linear fashion to do this, and then to do that, and then to do the next thing, and then the next thing. Well, this has all been compacted now. So it may not be run in a very logical, linear fashion. But if you allow yourself to be in the moment, you will know Dear Ones.

Our host has had many experiences of doing something in the last second and not knowing why. But all of a sudden when she has done it, then that has been revealed to her. And it is never always what you think it is. Actually most times it is never what you think it is. There is always something grander going on that gets revealed to you at a much later time. So trust your heart, Dear Ones, trust each other Dear Ones. Send that love out to those who are struggling and to yourself. Understand that struggle is part of the process and as you can get more and more comfortable with that and do it from the love of yourself and the love in your heart for others, the path will get easier. You will have much more moments of peace, of calm, of harmony and of being able to give what it is you already know in your heart.

So we leave you with that message, with those energies and knowing in your heart that this is a very effectual time that is happening and you are a very grand part of it as these times and energies intersect within your bodies, within your mind, within your heart and within your Spirit. So your Spirit is fully integrated at this time of great expansion. We leave you now with much honor for the path you've been on and joy in our hearts to be part of your process. We leave you now.

~.~.~.~.~.~.~.~.~.~.~.~.

Key Points:

- *There are many intersections of time and energy that have a great impact on all of the other dimensions. And it is all of these different crisscrosses of energies, of intersections, of beings, from all of the dimensions that are allowing your earth to ascend, to raise her vibration. And as you raise the vibration within your physical bodies, you are also helping Mother Earth to ascend.*

- *As you raise your awareness, you bring many along with you because there are great quantum leaps happening. Your physical reality is actually shifting molecularly. You have been working many eons at a mind level and it is now time to allow it to come through your physical bodies. As you make choices in this time intersection frame, it actually is changing the molecules.*

- *You are going through a great rewiring process that is balancing the right and left hemispheres of your brain so that they are working more in unity rather than in separation. The body is the assimilation method, it is the vehicle for the integration of all this beautiful knowledge and knowing that you have to be able to apply it in your life.*

- *You are receiving much Angelic support, much cosmic support, much support from all of the Masters in all of the different realms at this time to assist your process. It is just a matter of allowing, of allowing those energies, of allowing the love to support you.*

- *Whatever it is you are doing, do it from your joy. From that place all will be revealed, the next step, the next stage, the next action will be revealed to you because as we said, our message at this time for you is about THIS intersection of time and energy.*

September 11 - Infusion of Multi-Dimensional Energies
(Ojai, CA)

Dearest Beautiful Beings of Light,

We are the United Souls of Heaven and of Earth and it always brings us great delight to be in the presence of Light Beings. And we say this term with great emphasis because even though you hear that word, even though you have read those words, even though there have been many Masters tell you that you are Divine, that you are made of Light, it is now time, Dear Ones, to feel it; to feel the transformations that are going on within your physical being; to feel and be aware and acknowledge those transformations that are going on in your intelligence, in your mind, in your mental field.

There are many things that are happening within all of the bodies that are encompassed within being a human being: your physicality, your emotionality, your mentality and your spirituality. They are all being worked on at the same time.

You have gone through many phases, Dear Ones, of working on specific things only. So there may have been a health issue that you personally were working on through your own self-awareness, through connections with your medical system, through connections with your alternative system or there may have been an emotional issue that came up in your life that you needed help with or that you talked to a friend about or you went to a therapist about.

There were great periods of time that were allocated for clearings at certain levels. There was through the 70s, the 80s and into the 90s, a great time of psychotherapy and psychoanalysis and things that helped your mental awareness and cognizance and your emotional connection to that, and there have been times you have gone through very physical transformations, and then there have been times that you have gone through very immense spiritual enlightenments. And Dear Ones, now it is happening all at the same time.

So it is no wonder that you are feeling confused, disillusioned, concerned, unsettled. There are many terms that you have used in your descriptions, and we are here to assure you that we are very well aware of it and you have much support in all of the dimensions. And we say this continuously to our own host because she has really questioned the process that she has been through lately, and wondering if she is creating them herself or if she needs to take a physical action or if there is something that she needs to do. And we assure you there are many things that are going on within your physical body that are purely energetic. They are re-wiring and re-transformation for the transcendence of your physicality out of this denseness of your 3D world.

And yes, Dear Ones, if you feel guidance to seek medical assistance, please do so. It is important that you understand what is the best avenue for you. So we are not saying just to sit in your pain and allow. You are very strong transmitters of the energy at this point, that is moving through your bodies and our host had the opportunity last night in conjunction with her host of her home to be able to get some clarity and it is important that you get together with others of same vibration.

And that is critical, Dear Ones, to be in similar vibration. If you choose to stay in lower vibration, that is the information you are going to receive. If you choose to be in vibration that is not in sync with you on any level, whether it is higher or lower, forward, backward, there is no better or worse, it is what works and what does not work, what matches and what does not match with you. And again our host had a pretty difficult decision on September 9th to make around a family member because of feeling she should do something and knowing that it was not a vibrational match. And it was a very tough decision and we honor her for the choice that she made against things that she felt she should do. And as you make those choices for yourself, Dear Ones, much more energy will open up within your beingness.

You have allowed much energy to be drained from you through your mental processes of confusion, of doubt, of worry, of guilt, of all those things that you have been taught were important. And Dear Ones, they are not important. They are drains on your energy. Any time that you are feeling guilty about something, any time you are feeling remorseful about something, any time you are feeling your "shoulds" and your "have to's," you have heard this many, many times from many Masters and it has come to a critical point at this time that each time you tap into one of those energies, you are lowering your vibration. And at this time, your physical body is really needing you to keep your vibration high to assist the transition and the transmutation that it is going through at this time.

And it is all part of your thought process. Our host became very aware and has been really following the patterns of when a thought pattern comes in that is not serving her. Her body goes into immediate reaction. It used to be a "sort of" reaction before and now it is immediate. It tightens up and there is a wave of energy that moves through, that senses fear and there is a hot flash that goes with it and there is a purification that happens and as she becomes aware of what that thought was in the moment, then it clears.

So we are inviting you at this time Dear Ones to be very aware of your thought processes. It is your thought processes, your intentions, your awarenesses, your openness to possibilities, your gratefulness, your appreciation, your love, your joy, and again, Dear Ones, we know you have heard this many times and we are just reiterating because it is important for not only your mind to hear but your body to get it.

That is our mission with you: it is to keep saying the words, to help keep working with the energy of alignment for you so that it can feel good within your physical bodies.

You are not on this Earth to suffer, Dear Ones. You are not here to suffer mentally or emotionally or physically or spiritually. You are here for all of these beautiful forms to come in alignment with each other, right now, at this time. And you have a choice in that. You ARE the catalyst. You ARE the co-creators. You ARE all that it is necessary for that to happen for you first and foremost and then that does reverberate into everything else that you know and even to everything else that you do not know. Because there is very much happening for you at this time that you really do not know, Dear Ones, that you have not had the pleasure or the joy or the awareness of yet, that will be coming to you in the very near future at a Famous Players Theatre near you. (laughter)

It is, Dear Ones, time to start seeing it on the big screen. It is not any more fleeting thoughts or little visions or little mystical experiences that are going to be happening to you. You are now going to see this on the big screen, the big screen of you and the Universe and your connection to that Universe, to your Universe; your Universe from within, your Universe from without, the connection to all that is. So pay attention to what is passing by you on your big screen. There are many bits and pieces that are being given to you at this time through inspiration, through kinetic experiences, through synchronicities, through connections with others, through being placed in a certain geographical location to have a connection with a certain sound or music. There are so many factors and influences that are converging at this time, Dear Ones, and that is why you are feeling overwhelmed. That is why you are feeling confused. It truly, truly is happening at once.

Up until this time, it was a much gentler process, a much slower integration, a much... You had time to get an awareness and deal with it and then start to live it. Now it is happening so quickly and so much at once, we would like to really reassure you that it is okay, that you are capable, you have all the tools necessary, you have all the support necessary with each other as well as within all of the other dimensions.

And as you choose to live in that truth, to live in that grace and divinity of who you are, to co-create that space of serenity and consciousness around you in whatever way you need to do that, Dear Ones. And we know that many of you are having the experience of wanting to be in seclusion and wanting to create your own teeny little environment where nothing else influences you and that is okay for the moment but there will come a time when you are feeling much more fully integrated, much stronger physically, much more cognizant and aware of the bigger picture, again that full screen view of the movie, that you will be ready to step out, Dear Ones.

For right now is the process of, we wanted to say training but that is not the word. It is infusion. That is our message for you today. It is about infusion . . . of all of these energies that are allowing your co-creation, that knowing to come through at every cell of your body, every atom, every molecule that already knows all of this, it is being activated at this time and the infusion of all of the different awarenesses, knowings, wisdoms, integrations, all of this, there are so many words to describe things that are happening to you all at once and it is a magnificent process if you allow yourselves to just stay in the center.

We have been showing our host this image of a wheel like a wagon wheel and she has used it to describe what is happening for many of you. It is like all of the things you have ever done in your life ever, or in many lives, all the experiences are on the perimeter of this beautiful wheel with many, many, many spokes coming into the center. Some of them are big strong wooden ones, some of them are iron or metal ones, some of them are very teeny filament thread ones, and it depends on what that experience or information was and how you have been conduited, conducted to the middle of this circle, where you are the hub.

You are the axle. You are the center. You are the center of the Universe, Dear Ones. The center of the Universe runs through your body. And as you stay in that center and allow all of this infusion of energy to come to you it will be much easier than all of the grappling and searching and seeking and trying that you have been doing up to this point. Know, Dear Ones, it is up to you.

As you stay in your center and allow all of these beautiful infusions of energy experiences and support to move with grace and ease in a beautiful choreographed pattern as it comes in to you, through this infusion of energy to your core, to the hub of who you are, to that center of your "I Am" presence, to that flame of your Divine Essence. It is a beautiful analogy for you, Dear Ones, to see that that is the whole and as all of these energies come in to your core and it starts a rotation, a rotation that actually has been happening for a very long time but it is starting to take greater momentum now. It could be described in your terms as the Wheel of Fortune.

It is time, Dear Ones, for you to experience that Wheel of Fortune. Each time that you open to and allow yourself those possibilities, there is more probability that it will happen for you. Each time that you start to send your energies back outward through that wheel, you will lessen the strength of those possibilities. Allow all of these beautiful experiences, energies, knowings, wisdom and support to come into you to create that strength, that strength from within.

Take a breath, Dear Ones, and allow yourselves to feel that. Feel the infusion. Feel the infusion of many dimensional energies within your physical being. They are energies from your beautiful Mother Earth, your Gaia that are being given to you in great velocity and there are energies that are coming from all the different dimensions. There are energies that are coming from all the Masters that at one time walked on your beautiful Earth and there are the energies of all of the other dimensions that have never had the thrill of walking on your Earth. They are all working in harmony at this time for the greater good of the All, and you Dear Ones are at the hub of that. So as you breathe, allow yourself to feel that. It does not have to be overwhelming even though many of you are allowing that to happen in your awareness.

In your stillness you are able to receive the most. And in that stillness you receive the higher perspective. In that stillness all of this beautiful movement in the wheel is able to have a greater impact. And it does not take muscle power, it does not take mental power, it does not take emotional power, it just takes being in your own knowing, in your own stillness and allowing the infusions of these multi-dimensional energies to support you in this next awareness, this next bump in consciousness, this next bump in evolution.

It is imminent. It is right in front of your nose, Dear Ones. It is at your fingertips. It is in your heart. So as you open to these probabilities and possibilities and these opportunities for yourself, you will feel a sense of joy. And it is in that sense of joy that you will experience greater awarenesses of all of the newness that is being dropped into your dimension through the human being, through the human biology.

Even though we talked about all this infusion of energy coming in, the next part of the vision is also as it comes into the center, Dear Ones, it is being funneled and spouted outward from that hub of the wheel into all of the Cosmos.

Remember it is all one, it is all connected. There are many forms of energy within all of this and you are one very specific form of it but it is this coming into you and coming out from you and going out and coming back in. It is always a continuous flow of energy, of love, of joy, of centeredness, of peace, of harmony, and the more and more Dear Ones, that you can tap into and keep your core in those energies, the more you will see the magnificence of what is about to happen...to happen for you personally, for what is about to happen to Mother Earth and for what is about to happen in your Universe, in your Cosmos.

So Dear Ones it is always with great pleasure that we are able to share our words with you and we are able to help with the activation of that energy at your cellular level and to assure you that you are powerful beyond means and as you sit in your center in your hub and allow the energies, the infusion of the energies of the multi-dimensional you, you will have very great awarenesses of the truth of who you are and who each other is.

So sit in community as often as possible, Dear Ones, sit in groups even if it is only two, create as many opportunities as possible for you to be the catalyst for this infusion of the multi-dimensional energies within the physicality, within the 3D realm because it is about living it right now in your realm, not having to leave or do anything different than you are doing other than being, than letting it be so within you, that truth of who you are.

So open yourselves, Dear Ones, to the infusion of the multi-dimensional energies. Allow yourselves to turn on that screen, that beautiful movie screen to see the movie of the new world that is being created by you.

We leave you now, with great love in our heart, compassion for your journey, and honor for the Light that you carry, the Light that you are, and the Light that you shine now.

~.~.~.~.~.~.~.~.~.~.~.~.

Key Points:

- *You are made of Light; it is now time to feel it. Be aware and acknowledge the transformations that are happening within all of the bodies that are encompassed within being a human being: your physicality, your emotionality, your mentality, and your spirituality. There are many things that are going on within your physical bodies that are purely energetic. They are being re-wired and re-transformed for the transcendence of your physicality out of this denseness of your 3D world.*

- *You are very strong transmitters of energy. It is important that you get together with others of same vibration. Sit in community, sit in groups even if it is only two. Your physical body needs you to keep your vibration high to assist the transition and the transmutation that it is going through at this time.*

- *Be very aware of your thought processes, your intentions, your awarenesses, your openness to possibilities, your gratefulness, your appreciation, your love, your joy because it is important for not only your mind to hear but your body to get it.*

- *There will come a time when you are feeling much more fully integrated, much stronger physically, much more cognizant and aware of the bigger picture.*

- *In your stillness you are able to receive the most. And in that stillness you receive the higher perspective. Allow the infusions of these multi-dimensional energies to support you in this next awareness, this next bump in consciousness, this next bump in evolution.*

October 11 - Past, Present, Future Overlay
(Carlsbad, CA - Canadian Thanksgiving Day)

Dearest Beautiful Beings of Light,

We are so delighted to be with you this day. This beautiful day of gratitude, of thanksgiving, of appreciation, of giving, of receiving, of harvesting, of feeling that fulfillment of being fed, of being supported. It is a beautiful energy and we are so grateful to be part of your consciousness, of your awareness, that you have come together at this point in time to share your beautiful energy with each other. And we want to acknowledge that that is truly what it is about.

Yes, you think that you have come to connect with your friend Judith and to share in her offerings and to hear the message that we have for you and yes, that is a very beneficial and viable part of this gathering and this connection, but Dear Ones, we really want you to get that it is YOUR energy that makes the difference. Our host and "US" could speak until doomsday, but until we actually have someone who is willing to receive the words, who is willing to receive the activation, who is willing to integrate that in their lives, it means nothing. It is just energy floating out in the Cosmos.

But first of all, because our host is willing to be the conduit, to be the anchor and to be the spokesperson and to be the activator and transmitter for this wonderful energy that we have to share with you, that starts a whole process of energy. What do we want to call it? It's energy, there's more to it than activation, it is much bigger than that, Dear Ones, but it is the first step in the process. So by you connecting with our host and with "US," you have amplified it not 10 times, not 100 times, not 1,000 times: there isn't actually a number in your consciousness and awareness that could define how the energy gets amplified because you chose this day and this time to bring YOUR beautiful energy to the mix. (Pause)

And we take the pause for you, Dear Ones, to get it. We talk about this all the time. It is so important for you to get it. Get it in your mental awareness, get it in your physical body, get it in your heart center, to get it so that it is such a deep knowing and way of being that you never doubt it ever again in this existence. And when we talk about this existence it is not just what you are living in this body right now. We love the conversations at the beginning because as you know, we are available at all times through our host and when that intention is set, you are all receiving it.

So the conversations at the beginning are always so delightful for us because you are already tapping into "US." You are already receiving the words, the energy, the thoughts, the love and all of the compassion that we have for you. So your discussions at the beginning are you sensing the energy already and what our message is. And it really is about the overlaying of the past, the present and the future all happening at once and the awareness that you have that you can change either/or.

You are having very direct experiences now of this. Of creating new in this moment and also re-creating past so that it is new in this moment. And, Dear Ones, that is only the tip of the iceberg. This alignment of this day of the 11th of the tenth month is just following the alignment of yesterday, which was the 10:10.

And our host became very aware of that alignment of 10:10 last year and did a beautiful channel and so as she channels this energy on the 11th it is incorporating that beautiful energy of the 10:10 which is new beginnings.

One, Dear One, is always your new beginning and when you put it together with the zero of the ten, that zero contains the All. So look at the power in that alignment of the previous day of two 10:10's, two beginnings, two creations from the All that now are moving into the day of the 11th of Mastery.

So, Dear Ones, pay attention to your numerology, pay attention to your symbology, pay attention to what is being shown to you in many, many ways. You are getting guidance from so many realms now. It used to be just your own personal guides, or your Angels, or your Enlightened Beings but it is coming at you now from so many directions. It is one of the reasons that you are feeling disoriented and confused and not sure of who you are or what to do. And that is okay, Dear Ones, it is going to clarify. We assure you that it is all clarifying, for you. It is just this over stimulation right now of multi-dimensional energies. And if you go back and listen to the channels that we have given you in the previous weeks and months, you will see all the messages that are lining up for this time, this time now and the times to come in the next weeks and months and even the next few years.

There is a progression happening here for you, for your awareness, for your sustainability in this physical 3D world. And we always acknowledge that we have great compassion because we know it is not always easy. Our host has experienced some very intense physical symptoms through this transition. We always are assuring her that it is okay but it is very hard for her living in a physical body that is not comfortable as she is going through these transitions. So, Dear Ones, as you are all going through these transitions and you are the transmitters of the Great Light that you already are. And yes, it is coming from the Cosmos, and yes, it is coming from your Mother Earth, it is moving through your body. But, Dear Ones, it is your choice to be the transmitter. (Pause)

Again we take that pause so you can to feel it. Feel that truth in your body, feel that truth in your heart, feel that truth in your mind, Dear Ones. You are the transmitters of the light, you are the place holders now on Earth anchoring it for your Mother Earth. You are, we want to call it, the spouts or the fountains of this beautiful energy going out to the Cosmos so that we are also in the outer dimensions experiencing that beautiful light of yours as well. It is supporting us and we have said that many times as we spoke of at the beginning, our words, our energy would not be beneficial if there were not those of you to receive it.

So in this day of appreciation, gratitude and thanksgiving we are giving that to you, Dear Ones. So our message to you is encompassing all of the past, the present and the future. The message is to be in gratitude and appreciation for it all, every little piece, every little emotion, every little experience, every person that has ever crossed your path. Whether you felt they have supported you or whether they have demeaned you, it matters not, Dear Ones. It only matters that you transmute it. That you integrate the beauteousness of each interaction in your life. Whether it was on a very person level or where it has affected you deeply and emotionally or whether it was very distant that you may not even have been very aware of, but will now come into your awareness, into your realm, to have great impact on you. So it is about understanding, that as you integrate this truth of who you are, as you truly stand in your grandness, in your Divineness, in your light, all of these things that may have seemed bad, uncomfortable, traumatic or however you label them, are coming into wholeness. (Pause)

Again we take the pause for your mind to filter the information into your heart and into your body. This is what it is about, Dear Ones, it is living the truth in your body. And to be able to integrate that so that it serves you. It serves you in a way that you can now create from this new and empowered place. From the new ideas that can now drop in because you are clearing your perceptions of the past. And we really emphasize that word "perceptions" because, Dear Ones, and we are so grateful for your beautiful being who talked about her past, because it really was only her perception, and as each of you share your perception of your past and allow that to clear and to be moved into the now, you are able to now create a future that has much more cooperation, working together so there is not this separation because he did that, or she did that, or he said that, or they said that.

It is all irrelevant, Dear Ones, because it was only your perception. It is not necessarily the other person's perception. So as you are able to be in your truth and love yourselves in this moment, you will see grand shifts. First of all in the core of your own being that then, Dear Ones, reverberates out into everything that you think about, everything you say, everything you do, everything you touch, everything you experience.

So it is very important at this time, Dear Ones, for you owning that truth of who you are. For not being afraid to step forward and express yourself and to own whatever that truth is for you, but also, Dear Ones, allowing others to express their truth and to own their truth, because it may not look like yours, it may not feel like yours, Dear Ones. It is this coming together right now of all of the realities and there is no one reality that is right, there is no one reality that is wrong, it is all part of the same hologram, it is all connected.

85

We have said this many times, Dear Ones, about your interconnection with each other. So as you judge another for doing something wrong or for not understanding and supporting you, you are actually creating a disconnection that all of us are working in the other dimensions to help you to re-create those connections; the connection with yourself, those connections with each other. That does not mean, Dear Ones, that you have to be in each other's presence or you have to be so interconnected in each other's lives that it is uncomfortable, but there is a fine filament of energy that is connecting everything. So as you are clearing for yourself and then sending out these beautiful emanations, they are these beautiful, tiny little filaments of energy to other persons, to situations, to inanimate objects, to the cosmos, to the earth.

You are just at the threshold, Dear Ones, of understanding how powerful you are. And as you live in your truth, as you live in your bliss, as you live in your joy, as you live in your own integrity for owning who you are, you give permission for all others to do that, you emanate that out so they get it no matter what. And as you accept where each person is in their journey, first of all it makes it more comfortable for you. Our host had a great experience as she always does when she is back with her family, of just accepting who each and every one of them is and whatever behaviors they are needing to express in the moment. And for allowing them that space; that it is just where they are in their process of evolution and the only person that you are truly responsible for, Dear Ones, is yourself.

And when you do that for yourself, we take it back to show you that as you do that for yourself you change the past, you create the future. A future that may have been because you were in angst, or pain, or resentment, or hurt has now been changed because you have allowed yourself to be in that place of forgiveness, in that place of acceptance, in that place of knowing, in that place of just being in that place of just living. And we want to really exaggerate that word "living" because many of you are aware of past lives. You are tuning now into future lives, but it is in the living of it, not in the thinking of it, it is not in the emotions of it, it is in the true essence of living in each moment that you bring forth these energies that are creating the great shift. So as you are moving between these realities of past, present and future, Dear Ones, see it as the Hologram. See it as you can take any part of it and create the hologram, the wholeness, the wholeness of who you are, the wholeness of who we all are, that wholeness, that Allness of the oneness. It is all compacted, (hmm - not compacted?), all IN that Oneness, that Oneness of the hologram of past, present and future.

And your scientists, Dear Ones, are going to make great strides in the next few years in understanding that, that part of the hologram that you already are. And for those of you who have a gift, the gift of intuitiveness, the gift of knowing, you are going to be shown much over the next few years, Dear Ones, that will be of great assistance for those that are not quite there yet, that are having experiences that they do not know how to express or they do not know how to comprehend them. So all of you have been prepared at this time and that is why you are called to being in our energy and hearing our words, the energy of the Mastery, the energy of being your Divinity.

Because there will be many, Dear Ones, that come to you and your words will soothe them, your words will support them, your words will empower them. And as we say words, the energy that is coming out is "worlds." There are many worlds at this time, Dear Ones, that are coming together in your awareness. Not just your 3D world. There are many worlds around you, below you, through you, that are coming together at this time in your holographic memory that you will be able to access that information when it is necessary, when it is needed, whether it be in a conversation with another being or whether it be energy that you exude to the Cosmos, Dear Ones. Remember it is all a giving and receiving, a back and forth, a to and fro. And as long as you are in that flow and you do not go into your fear and stop it, there will be much gratification for you and fulfillment.

And even though it may feel like you are in a void or an unknowing at this time, Dear Ones, just be with it because there is much. There is much that is being prepared for you in a method that will be able to be comprehended by you at this time as you move forward in your spiritual evolution. As you are open to knowing that you are way more than what you have been told, as you are able to truly incorporate and feel that Divinity, that essence, that cosmetology of everything that ever has been, ever is and ever will be in this now moment. (Pause)

And again we take the pause for that to filter from your mind through your heart and into your body and for it to really anchor and not for your mind to take it into overwhelmment. "Oh my god, that sounds so big, it sounds so immense, it sounds so over stimulating, how could I as one little being on Earth, one physical being possibly comprehend or do whatever it is that is being prepared for little old me?" And we tell you, Dear Ones, it is because you are not alone. You may see yourself as one single being, but you truly are not. You are everything, you are everyone.

When our host asks about "US," we always tell her, we are you and you are "US" and we are All. We are everything. So the same applies to each of you, Dear Ones. When you go in your question mode and you wonder how am I going to do this, how am I going to reach people, how am I going to change the world, how am I going to help shift the problems in my world.

It is not about the how. You know that, Dear Ones. You have been told that many times. It is about being your Divine Essence. It is about living it, it is about knowing that the past, present and future are all happening at the same time. And as you stay in that place, you have a lot of clarity, you have a lot of power, you have a lot of energy and you know exactly what action to take next. So it is not about just sitting in meditation and allowing all this wonderful energy to move through your body to feel. It is really at a time now, as you learn to integrate your full spirit into the physical biology, that you will be very clear on what to do, what action steps to take. And it is happening for you as those of you expressed at the beginning and it will happen in increments. So there will be great boosts that will happen and you will know without a shadow of a doubt what your next step is. And then you will get there and wonder what is next.

So it is not always going to be a forward motion, Dear Ones. The rhythms of the Universe do not always move in the same direction. They ebb and they flow so always when you are in the process, accept the process of what is because there is so much happening for you at once. There are many, many, many, many, many, many layers happening energetically all at the same time.

So as you get your mind and your awareness around the fact that it is holographic, you will have a much deeper understanding and inner peace of how to be in that. So, Dear Ones, we honor you and your logical, mental processes and are here to help you to shift some of that through your body, so that yes you can still use your logical, analytical processes but to be in the flow of that beautiful harmony. The harmony of the whole that it is all working together no matter what it looks like in your external world. When something comes up that feels challenging, discordant, unsettling, give it thanks. Know that it is moving you, it is moving you out of the denseness, it is moving you out of the old paradigms, out of the old thinking.

And as you give it more gratitude, it will move that much more quickly and it will not have such a grip on you. So, Dear Ones, be grateful for any challenge that is showing up in your life and you will see it disperse very quickly because you are giving great intent to yourself, first of all, and to the Universe for much support at this time, and to know that we are here for you on all levels whether it be "US," whether it be the other Ascended Masters, whether it is Angels, whether it is Guides, whether it is Star Beings.

There are so many in many, many dimensions at your service at this time. So take that in, Dear Ones, through your mind, through your heart, through your physical being and know that is the truth for you at this time: that as you are experiencing the past, present and future in the now, there is much Cosmic, Universal, Angelic support for you to move through that process of integration to create the New World.

We leave you now with great honor and joy in our hearts to be part of your activation, your integration and your moving forward. We love you dearly and we leave you now.

~.~.~.~.~.~.~.~.~.~.~.~.

Key Points:

- *The past, the present and the future are all happening at once and you can change any of it. You are having very direct experiences of creating new in this moment and re-creating the past.*

- *You are the transmitters of the Great Light that you already are. It is moving through your body. You are at the threshold of understanding how powerful you are! You can now create from this new empowered place. From the new ideas that can now drop in because you are clearing your perceptions of the past.*

- *Encompassing all of the past, the present and the future, the message is to be in gratitude and appreciation for it all, every little piece, every little emotion, every little experience, every person that has ever crossed your path. Accept where each person is in their journey. As you do that for yourself, you can change the past and you create the future.*

- *There are many worlds around you, below you, through you, that are coming together at this time in your holographic memory that you will be able to access information when it is necessary. Know that the harmony of the whole is all working together no matter what it looks like in your external world. There is no one reality that is right, there is no one reality that is wrong; it is all part of the same hologram, it is all connected.*

- *As you are experiencing the past, present and future in the now, there is much Cosmic, Universal, Angelic support for you to move through that process of integration to create the New World.*

November 11 - "11-11-11"
Portal for Integration & Utilization
(Ojai, CA)

Dearest Beautiful Beings of Light,

We are the United Souls of Heaven and of Earth. And it brings us great delight, great joy and expands our love in even greater capacity to be in the presence of Lightworkers, light beings, light senders, light transmitters. This, Dear Ones, is what you are. You are the conduits for all of the beautiful energy that is being anchored on your beautiful Gaia, on your earth, on your planet. It is through the human medium, the human physiology, you are the conduits. It is through your feelings, through your words, through your actions, through your thought and just through your energy field that much of the transformation of what you call the Great Shift is happening.

It is not an event that is going to just flip on a certain date or a certain time. It has been a process of many years that is being accelerated at this time through your awareness, through your intent, through your consciousness, through your willingness. And we are in great awe and great honor for the processes that each and every one of you have been through to bring you to this point in time. This intersection of time and energies is a portal. It is a portal of integration, it is a portal of application, it is a portal of action, of really moving forward and seeing the abundance, seeing the rewards of your efforts at this time.

And even though there will be challenges, it is part of your human dimension, of strengthening your awareness of your spirit, of your body, of all of the above, so that it works in harmony for you to stay in your center, in your groundedness as many things unfold very quickly. Each and every one of you is experiencing the intensification and the amplification of energies as they are converging at this time because they are coming from many places. They are coming to you from your beautiful Mother Earth. They are coming to you from your Angelic Kingdom. They are coming to you from your Natural Kingdom, from your Animal Kingdom, from the Universe, from the Cosmos. It is never ending, the amounts of energy that you are receiving at this time.

And Dear Ones, it is up to you how you receive them, how you integrate them, and therefore, how you utilize them. And that is a key word in our message to you this day is through this portal of integration, how are you going to utilize the great gifts, the great support and the energies that you are receiving at this time from everything? Everything, everyone, every object, every being seen and unseen. There is this huge conglomeration of everything, of the all happening all at once.

And this, Dear Ones, is contributing to part of your confusion. And we know that many of you are in places of questioning at this time of what is next. And we really encourage you, Dear Ones, to stay in your center. Because there will be chaos around you. There will be chaos in your home life, there can be chaos in your work life, there can be chaos in your community life, there can be chaos in your global world. But Dear Ones, it is up to you how you, first of all perceive that, and how you stay within your own center and then allow that reverberation to go out so it actually shifts whatever challenges or chaos that may be in your external world.

There is a time coming of great change, the change has been building over a number of decades and it is coming to a point at this time, as our host spoke earlier, of the birthing and the birthing may get messy and that is okay, Dear Ones. Know that it is all happening in divine orchestration and you, Dear Ones, are the ones who are orchestrating it. (Pause)

And we take the pause for that information to filter from your mind through to your body. Because it is about owning it, Dear Ones. It is about stepping into that truth of your empowerment. You are the ones that are orchestrating all of this through your thoughts, through your intentions, through your heart, through your love. There are many of us in the other realms that are supporting you to do this, to be all that you can be. So it is at this time we are encouraging you to let go of the gunk, to let go of the past, no matter what has happened in the past. And yes, this has had a great influence on you psychically, emotionally, and physically. There have been many things affecting the molding of who you are, but Dear Ones, you get a choice in all that now.

92

You have moved beyond many influences in your physical realm and as you take that into your awareness and into your consciousness that you no longer have to be affected, whether it be by the astrology, whether it be by the environment, whether it be by another person's perception of you, whether it be by a great change in your physical circumstance that you have the power Dear Ones, to utilize these moments and incidences to your greater good which then, of course, is to the greater good of all.

So as each of you step into your empowerment, into your Divinity, into that truth of who you are, know that all is well, know that you are being taken care of no matter what. That as you connect on that resonant field that is being set for you as a beautiful Lightworker it is there for you even though you may not see it, you are feeling it. We can guarantee you that you are feeling the resonance of the light field that has been set for you for the integration, the application and the utilization to create the world that you desire, the world that you know to be true, the world where all live in harmony, where all live in cooperation, where all live in co-creation with each other that then creates the whole.

There are many things going on behind the scenes at this time that will automatically be put in place, Dear Ones, when the shell cracks, so to speak, when all the hardened mud around your world, around your consciousness falls away, there are many structures that have already been put in place by many enlightened people.

There has been work being done through you and for you on your earth, first of all since the beginning of time but more recently in the last few decades that all of a sudden will open up like a beautiful scene being projected onto a screen of what is possible for you as individuals, for you as families, for you as communities and for you as countries, for you as a global community, for you as a Universal community.

We keep showing you the layers of what is possible, but it begins from within, Dear Ones. It begins with your every thought, it begins with your every word, it begins with your every action and that is coming from a place of self-honoring, of true love for yourself, a true love for humanity, and most of all, Dear Ones, of joy.

So as you open this day on the 11:11:11, Dear Ones, take in the visual of that alignment. See the first "11" and the second "11" and the third "11." It is a number line up of ones, and that one is you, and that one is the whole. But look at how they are standing beside each other. The one of you, and the one of the whole of the oneness are standing beside each other. And what is happening as you are aware of that, is the integration. It will not be about separation anymore. It is not about you and the other, or you and the whole, it is about you within it. You as a whole being reverberating out the wholeness to the wholeness, to the Oneness. And it is all really quite a dichotomy of energy in a metaphor that is actually very interesting if you sit with it, Dear Ones, and feel it.

We have given information in a previous channeling on the "11" about it being a wave of, and we called it a Light Army at the time, but there is a better word for it that was given through our host and her host the previous evening, about being "agents."

It is about this beautiful alignment of each and every one of you standing straight up, owning who you are, expressing who you are and being the agents of light for the change that is happening no matter what. And as you hold that light within yourselves, Dear Ones, as you ground it into the earth, as you receive it from the Cosmos, as you bring it back up from the Earth to the Cosmos to us, to all of us in all of the different realms who are seeing you at this time, it is a beautiful collaboration of light, of love, of faith, of truth.

There is a beautiful saying that was given to you many decades ago about being the Light, the Truth, and the Way. And that is, Dear Ones, what you are right now. So take that into your being, take that into your consciousness, allow the activation for you at a cellular level so that you understand at a very physical, mental, emotional level and feel it in your body, of your Mastery. Those words that were spoken by one of your great Masters has been spoken many times in many ways in many languages, and you have given adoration and revered these beings and Masters, and it is now time, Dear Ones, to revere and to adore yourself. Because you are it. You are the Masters!

As you open this day to this portal of integration of these beautiful Mastery energies, what will happen in the next few weeks for you as you move through into the next portal, the December 11th and 12th, will be a very significant doorway of completion and opening all at the same time. It will happen very quickly and very simultaneously almost to the point where you will not even understand. It will be like this wave of energy that all of a sudden you have shifted and so much will change for you at that time, Dear Ones.

So as you stand in this beautiful Mastery energy and receive it this day at this time at this intersection, take a breath in Dear Ones, and give your intent and allow your being, your physical being, to feel it and to receive it at a deep core level, at your cellular levels. Breathe in, Dear Ones, and allow.

As you feel this activation, it is centered in your core, it is centered in your heart, it is centered in your empowerment center, it is centered in your emotional center, it is centered in your intuitive center, it is centered in everything that you are, everything that you say, everything you think, everything you express. And there is a great co-creation going on within the cells of your body at this time that will be activated for you to see now, to see physically at greater levels, to perceive things that you have not ever perceived or seen before.

There is an upgradement that is happening with all of your systems because of your choice to align with these energies this day, with the Mastery energies of the "11." And be very aware, Dear Ones, of each time that you see the symbol of an "11" anywhere. It might be on a clock, but it may be in nature. It may be two sticks lying on the ground parallel to each other. So think about as those ones line up in parallel, they are traveling a similar path at the same time.

And Dear Ones you are traveling this path with us. It is all happening at the same time. And as you travel that with "US" and with your own guides, with your own inspiration, with your own faith, with your own energies that are supporting you, Dear Ones, you are creating that amplification that we spoke about earlier in the channel. As you amplify it for yourself, you are amplifying it for everyone. It is a reverberation that is exponentialized by your intention, by your being, by your standing, by your grounding, by your giving, by your receiving, by your loving.

It is not as complex or complicated as you make it out to be, Dear Ones. We have said this many times: keep it simple, allow yourself to feel it from the inside. Each time that you get pulled off into what would be considered possibly not Mastery (which actually is your Mastery because it is of course, with each decision that you make to empower yourself from the circumstances that may not have felt empowering, that then you are actually in your Mastery. It is a big joke because you are in your Mastery all the time.) So even though we are using the word "Mastery" in helping for you to feel that in your body, Dear Ones, know that everything you do is your Mastery.

So as you bring that feeling, that knowing to everything you do, that is what you will experience. It does not matter whether it is something grandiose. We have said this many, many, many times in our channels and we will continue to say it. It does not matter what you do, it matters how you do it. So if you were only taking a drink of water, if you do it with great intention, if you do it in your centeredness, in your Mastery, that water then is the amplification of energy within your body. It matters not what you do, Dear Ones, it only matters how you do it. And this energy of the 11:11:11 alignment is allowing you to do it with greater ease. (Pause)

And again we take the pause for that information to filter from your mind through body, so you really get that, you feel it, that you are able to do this with ease.

You can struggle if you choose, Dear Ones, though it is no longer necessary. It is about connecting with each other and reflecting that ease back, that support, that cooperation to each other. Our hostess had wonderful, wonderful experiences of that in the very recent time the past few weeks of her traveling and connecting with people who just make it easy. Her being with them makes their life easier. Them being with her makes her life easier. It is how it is in the New World, Dear Ones.

So look for that ease in yourself first of all and share that with each other because that is part of the amplification that is being given to you at this day. As this portal of integration moves through your body, this opening, it is allowing the ease for what you are here now to do, to be, to allow. That beautifulness, that magnificence, that gloriousness, that joy, that beauteousness - we could go on and on, and on forever, Dear Ones, describing what we see in you.

It is now time for you not only to see it in yourself, but to feel it and to live it.

So, Dear Ones, we leave you with these words, with this energy, with the beautiful alignment of the 11:11:11 Mastery energy being assimilated through your physical being, for the integration, the application and the utilization for the co-creation of all that will come to you, from you, through you in the days to come.

With great honor, Dear Ones, we leave you now with joy in our hearts and awe for you for who you are. We leave you now at this time.

~.~.~.~.~.~.~.~.~.~.~.~.

Key Points:

- *This intersection of time and energies is a portal of integration, of application and of action, of really moving forward and seeing the abundance, seeing the rewards of your efforts.*

- *You are feeling the resonance of the light field that has been set for you to create the world that you desire. Know that you are being taken care of no matter what. There are many structures that have already been put in place by many enlightened people.*

- *The "11" is about being a wave of "Light Agents" standing straight up, side by side owning who you are and expressing that for the change that is happening.*

- *Between December 11th and 12th will be a very significant doorway of completion and opening all at the same time. There is an upgradement that is happening with all of your systems because of your choice to align with these energies this day, with the Mastery energies of the "11."*

- *It matters not what you do, it only matters how you do it. Being "the Light, the Truth and the Way" is what you are. Revere and adore yourself. As this portal of integration moves through your body, it is allowing the ease for what you are here now to do, to be, to allow. It is now time for you to feel it and to LIVE IT!*

December 11 - Orchestration of the New
(Ojai, CA)

Dearest Beautiful Beings of Light,

We are the United Souls of Heaven and of Earth. And it brings us great delight, as always, Dear Ones, to be in your presence. And we are emphasizing the YOUR, it is about YOU! We have spoken about this in many channels and now it is time to truly anchor that right now in this second, in this moment, through your bodies so that you are living it in each moment. You, Dear Ones, are the Masters. You Dear Ones, are what you are waiting for. You Dear Ones, have all you need at this time at this intersection of time and energy for moving forward in whatsoever you so desire. There is no more needing anything. There is no more waiting for anything. There is no more feeling like you do not have.

That is very old energy, Dear Ones. It is now about truly embracing that you have all that you need, that you are all that you are, that you are it, that you are anchoring this now into your 3-Dimensional realm. There is not so much separation anymore between the realms, between the dimensions because of all of the work that you have done on so many levels of your psyche, of your emotional bodies, of your physical bodies, of all of your awareness, your spiritual awareness. It is all coming together at this time in this beautiful orchestration of the wholeness of you.

So as we share these words and this energy with you, Dear Ones, really know that as your truth. It is the orchestration of the new and that is our message for you this day. It is all of this coming together in the beautiful symphony that you already are. It is just now that you are the conductor that comes in and lifts the baton and starts the beautiful melody. It is you, Dear Ones, that is the conductor, as well as the symphony, as well as each of the instruments. It is all happening at once. As you try to individuate each of those things, those are just analogies, but if you relate them to things in your life, as you individuate them, you fragment them and that is causing you the confusion in your lives at this time. So as you draw it all together, as all of the experiences that you have had, Dear Ones, all of

99

them, no matter what they have felt like, whether they have felt very insignificant or whether they have felt over the top traumatic, they were all serving you. And it has been a beautiful preparation to bring you, to you, to this point in time. (Pause)

And we take that pause, for the filtering, for the anchoring from your mind through your body. It is this point in time. It is very significant, Dear Ones, that you get this, that you feel this, that you live this. It is that orchestration of everything that ever was, or ever will be, has now converged right now through your physical bodies. And as you really allow yourselves to tune in to that harmony from within, that beauteousness of your physical body being the container for All That Is, for All That Ever Was and All That Ever Will Be, you will feel a fullness. And it does not have to be an overwhelmedness, it does not have to be a too fullness. It is just a beautiful fullness from within that you will now be able to use to create in your life, in your thoughts, in your awareness of all that is about to unfold. It is a great emerging, a birthing of many, many, many things that are new to your consciousness.

And so as you have emptied out and cleared many, many things in this past, and there are many of you on this call that have done a lot of clearing on many levels that it is now time to embrace this fullness that already is as well. So there is not a difference between the emptiness and fullness, it is all the same thing. So as you move forward in your lives, Dear Ones, embrace that knowing from within. The orchestration of what you are about to create has not ever been done. (Pause)

And again we take the pause for your minds to filter through that. And we can feel the tick, tick, tick, tick, tick, tick going on in your minds of, "What was that she just said? What was that - it has never been done?" It is such a brand new energy that you are embracing at this time, Dear Ones, that there is nothing, there is no precedent for it. It is brand new.

And as you can allow that, and not have to analyze, or clarify, or strategize anything that has to do with it, to just be open to this orchestration of the new. And we have referred to this a number of times before and just touched upon it briefly in other channels and we will continue to do so in other channels to come because as you are able to see those little specks, those sparks of the newness and feel them and allow that to expand within your beingness, there will be much "awareness" is the word that we are coming up with, but it is grander than that, Dear Ones. You know in your English language that there really are not the words yet to describe what is coming, what is possible and actually what is already here for you. It is just a matter of you stepping into it right now at this time, in this moment, in this NOW. You do not need to be looking forward to the future. Yes, there is much talk at this time of the 2012 and all of the things and theories that are going on around that, and yes, listen to it, open your mind to it, and listen to what resonates with you. But know, Dear Ones, that it is actually happening right now.

The linear time is still there for YOUR purposes. It is really not part of the whole Universe. It has been laid out for you to come to this point in time, for you to embrace the wholeness and the no beginning, no end, the infinity, the continuum of All That Is, All That Ever Was, and All That You Are now in this moment.

So allow yourselves, Dear Ones, to be open to what that is for you. And as you move into embracing that, to listening to the orchestration of the new . . . so when we use that word, the Orchestration means "happening," all of these things coming together all at once to create a Wholeness. That is the Oneness, the Wholeness that we have spoken of many times and that is YOU, Dear One, it is YOU.

There is no differentiation. You can lay it out in many terms, in many languages in many, many different things, but as you embrace that Orchestration of the New you will understand how you fit in to that, who you are and what you are in that Orchestration of all of the pieces, of all of the sounds, of all of the light, of all of the energy coming together at this time. It has been quite dispersed and for a great reason, because you were not ready. And now Dear Ones, you are ready.

There are many of you walking this Earth, who are now able to hold that fullness of your Being, to hold that fullness of your Spirit, to hold that fullness of your passions, to hold that fullness of your knowing, to hold that fullness, Dear Ones, of your Spirit, that Spirit that is fully integrating right now as we speak in your physical biology. And that has been our purpose in every word we have ever spoken to you, and every activation that you have felt through your body, and every word transcribed and written and read that comes through our host is for that full integration of that Divinity, of that Divine Essence of who you are. And as that is happening on a grander and grander scale, Dear Ones, this orchestration of the new will just happen with ease and grace. (Pause)

And again we take the pause. These are the key words, Dear Ones, the EASE and GRACE, the EASE and the GRACE. The orchestration of the new is possible through ease and grace. So take a breath, Dear Ones, and take that in through your physical senses, through your breath, through your ears, and right through your systems, through your energetic systems, through your nervous system, so that you can truly anchor that in your body. And as we speak we are doing work with your energetic bodies so you can more fully embody that, that trueness, that newness, that ALLness that you are.There is much work being done with you, Dear Ones, on a physical level so that you can truly embody all of this as you move into the coming year.

The year 2010 brings much awareness for all of you and many shifts, shifts of your physical cellular beingness, of your consciousness and it is being much more strengthened and connected with your Cosmic origins. So as you are open to that, Dear Ones, as you are fully embodying the Universe and allowing that to be shown to you through your cellular body, the Universe, Dear Ones, is contained within your cellular body. And it is that orchestration of that cellular body that is creating the resonant field for all of you to step into. You have already stepped into many layers and many aspects of this resonant field, and it is just now being bumped up to a greater resonance a greater frequency. That you are now able to, and we want to say "tap into" and that is not the word, it is to truly "embody" it, that is the word. It is the EMBODIMENT.

You can connect with Source Energy, you can connect with whatever teachings, philosophies, whatever suits you to stay in that place of your inner knowing, of your feeling.

Our host had an experience as she was traveling to Ojai, of a great emotional overwhelmment and she really questioned what was happening. Was it something she just thought, was it something she just experienced, was it something that she, you know, didn't do? She was doing all of these mental questions and judgments of herself and it was, Dear Ones, an experience of the immense, wonderful opportunities that are opening up through your physical bodies and through, Dear Ones, your energetic heart. That beautiful golden heart, that place within your being that started out as a teeny, little spark in your existence and has been growing, and growing and growing and expanding and growing to the point where it was almost impossible for your physical body to contain and because of all of the intentions you have set, Dear Ones, and called in help from the other realms, you have been open and allowing that help from the other realms to assist your physicality, and your mentality, and your emotionality, and your spirituality, to embrace this now.

And Dear Ones, we are here to affirm to you that this beautiful heart opening will serve you well. (Pause)

And again we take that pause to allow the information to filter from your mind through your body. The heart opening, Dear Ones, will serve you well. And again there are many ways that you can do that, there are many modalities, there are many situations, there are essences, and music, and vibration. There are so many ways, dance and art and music for you to allow that heart opening.

And Dear Ones, you can make it as complicated or as simple as you so choose. It is just in setting that intention to be in your own loving space, in your own open-hearted space that will create that for yourself. So the experience that our host was having was this beautiful opening of her heart that she equated with some sort of emotion that she has experienced in the past. She thought it was sadness, but it was actually not sadness. It was grandness. It was grandness of having the experience of the ALLness.

So as you do that for yourself, Dear Ones, allow the tears to flow. There is such an opening for you at this time of "Ahhhh!." And when you experience "Ahhhh!," there are many tears that may go with that because of you not having the experience of this before. So as you are opening to this orchestration, as you are present with it, and as you share it with others, there are so many minute things happening. And as you sit with another person and share your thoughts and your feelings and your emotions, it is validation that it is happening, that it is all very real.

And we spoke of this in our last channel with you, Dear Ones, about the real versus the unreal. And you get to choose what that is for you and how you embrace that in your own life. There was a wonderful comment from one of your participants about how she saw the spiritual world as real and she always had, whereas most of the comments were about the physical world. So Dear Ones, know that it is all orchestrating right now something new that you have not had the experience of before.

So as you step forward in each action in your life right now be aware, be aware of what is being shown to you, be aware of how you are thinking and speaking and what you are embracing and attracting into your own life at this time that will facilitate that orchestration of the NEW as YOU! The new and the you are intersecting at this time. For you to be part of that orchestration, for you to be the anchoring of that orchestration, for the Lightworkers and all of those that you touch so lovingly in your lives, to anchor this energy.

We are always in great honor and awe of you as the vessels, the conduits of this energy on your planet, on your beautiful Mother Earth, as you are the beings that are able to do this. We are only here in service to you, to you the Lightworkers, to you the Human Beings, to you the conduits of the beautiful light energy that is pouring in to your planet as we speak. And remember, Dear Ones, it is not only pouring in, it is also being given out through your physical body, through your words, through your music and sound and dance and art and lovingness. As you reverberate, all of this beautiful Divinity, this Divine Energy that is part of who you are, this orchestration of the new will be a seamless adventure as you move forward.

So Dear Ones, take in these words, the energy, the activation with the intent of the ease and the grace. And what we are here to help you shift in your consciousness and your awareness is the struggle, is the pain, is the overwhelmment, of the working too hard. Dear Ones, take in this energy and vibration of the orchestration of the new with ease and grace.

And we are going to add on the vibration "this is who you are." You are Beings of Joy, Beings of Love, and Beings of Light. And we leave you now at this time, Dear Ones, with those beautiful words and energy and knowing that you are the ones that are creating the New World, the orchestration of the New World that is in place for you right now as we speak. It is the embodiment of you as you step forward in the wonderful resonant field that is right there before your eyes.

So we leave you now with great love in our hearts and honor for your journey and with great support and service for you at this time. And we leave you now with great love in our hearts.

~.~.~.~.~.~.~.~.~.~.~.

Key Points:

- *Embrace that you have all that you need. You are the conductor that comes in and lifts the baton and starts the beautiful melody. The orchestration of everything that ever was or ever will be has now converged right now through your <u>physical bodies</u>.*

- *What you are about to create has not ever been done. It is such a brand new energy that you are embracing at this time that there is no precedent for it.*

- *The orchestration of the new is possible through EASE and GRACE. Listen to what resonates with you!*

- *The Universe is contained within your cellular body and it is that orchestration of that cellular body that is creating the resonate field for all of you to step into.*

- *As you reverberate, all of this beautiful Divinity, this Divine Energy that is part of who you are, this orchestration of the new will be a seamless adventure as you move forward.*

Afterward

My dear friend and editor, Carolyn, was reading the mini-channel that I sent out in my December 31st newsletter this morning and she said "This HAS to go into the "Your Mastery - Live It Now!" e-book. It is setting the stage for what is to come next and people need to see this!" She was so excited as she said it and we both got chills of electric energy move through our bodies, so we knew it was Divine confirmation.

Thank you Carolyn for being so tuned into the energy. I knew there was a reason why getting the e-book ready for the scheduled delivery date was not coming together as quickly as I had hoped and it was because this channel needed to be included.

So here you go . . . a little bonus to show you where we are headed in 2010 and beyond. "US" will have more teachings and wisdom to share as we go along. Stay tuned!

. . . Judith

Dearest Beautiful Beings of Light,

As you come to completion with the year 2009, a year of integration of Mastery energy, you are moving into a new "Decade of Light" unprecedented on your earth. This past year was about much transition, completion and integration. The year 2010 heralds the beginning of a whole new harmonics of vibration of the Light from within you.

The amplification of all your personal gifts, in whatever medium you choose to express them, will be very noticeable and applicable. There has been much preparation work done energetically on all levels for this next stage of your evolution. So rejoice in that knowing, share it with others and celebrate! Celebrate and acknowledge those gifts in yourself and all who you connect with. Those who stand before you and interact in your life in this coming year will emanate a love and radiance that will be breathtaking . . . and you are one of them! That is why we refer to you as Light Beings. That is not only what you are but who you are. You are the angels who have come to earth at this time to "be" the light, not just read about it or talk about it, but to live it and breath it.

The proverbial "light bulbs" moments will literally become the norm. You have shed so much density and negativity in the past decade that you will now truly experience your lightness within your physical body. You will actually see it in others with your physical eyes not just your inner vision. The depictions in your beautiful artwork of the glow around celestial beings was not a fantasy or imagination. It is very real and you all now have the physical capacity to clearly see it and emanate it. Your scientists and physicists are doing much to substantiate this phenomenon thereby making it more accepted in your mainstream world (not just within your spiritual communities) because your scientists are looked upon as having credibility and will reach those who need that validation. They have come as scientists into this realm at this time to prove and substantiate the spiritual and metaphysical events that will occur in greater proportions in this decade.

We have called this the "Decade of Light" because you have truly moved through the darkness and can embrace and embody your Light anytime you so choose with ease and grace. There is much support from the celestial and cosmic realms for you to do so. Sing your song, dance your dance, create your art, write your book, do whatever feeds your soul and infuse all you do with your Light and your love.

Emanate your luminosity and light up your world with joy!

In Love and Service,

"US"

Support for Integration of New Energies
Words of Wisdom from "US"

1. BREATHE!! *This is the absolute most important thing you can do for yourself. When you are concentrating on your breathing, you are not giving your energy to what you perceive might be wrong. Breathing gets you centered and allows you to feel your Divine Essence on the inside where "all is well." This is where you will receive your true guidance.*

2. THINK HAPPY THOUGHTS. *Sounds a little cliche, however if you remember the story of Peter Pan when he was teaching the children to fly, that is what he told them. As they did, they became lighter and lighter and were able to fly. And that is what you are doing, changing to a lighter vibration.*

3. NATURE. *Be in nature as often as possible. Let the nature spirits help infuse your physical body and rebalance it. Your bodies are going through much upgrading and the plants, the animals and the Earth herself are available to assist you.*

4. REST and QUIET TIME. *With all the energetic upgrading going on for you, it is important to be still and to sleep whenever possible. It is like a baby or teenager who is going through a growth spurt, they require lots of sleep. You are going through an immense spiritual growth spurt and sleep will facilitate a smoother transition. Even just sitting quiet allows your mind and body to relax to be more receptive to the higher vibrational energies.*

5. BE IN THE NOW. *Being present in the moment is vital to you being able to manage your energy. There is much chaos in the external world and as you are present to what you are doing in this very moment you have access to ALL of your energy rather than it being fragmented.*

6. DO THINGS THAT FEEL GOOD. *Old energies are being cleared from your mind, your body and from your cellular memory. As they come up in your everyday life, just acknowledge them and do something that feels good. It will clear out the gunk much faster.*

7. MOVEMENT and MUSIC. *Anything where you are moving your body and/or using your voice will accelerate the clearing of the density you have been carrying and makes space for the higher vibrational "you."*

8. WATER. *You are already well aware of the benefits of drinking high quality, pH balanced water. It will really support your bodies to conduct the new energy.*

9. NUTRITION. *Be aware of putting live food into your body and raising the vibration of anything else by infusing it with light energy through your thoughts, your vision and your intention. Consume all that you eat with great pleasure.*

10. LOVE and LIGHT. *Each time you have a loving thought or focus on the "light from within" you are embracing the new energies and therefore, emanating them into the world. This is the best gift you can give yourself or anyone.*

11. SHARE YOUR JOY. *That is the key to well being for yourself, for all others, for your planet and for the Universe. Share your joy in any and every way possible. Just BE it!*

About The Author

Judith Onley embraces and shares the gift of teachings being given to her through a group of non-physical spiritual teachers who call themselves "US," (United Souls of Heaven Earth) whose purpose in coming forth at this time is to activate the Divine Essence within all Human Beings. She also empowers people through movement, dialogue and energy work to realize their full potential.

Through her role as a channel, metaphysical teacher, Reiki Master and energy balancing practitioner, she encourages awareness of subtle physical, mental, emotional and spiritual factors that may be influencing well-being. She also provides leadership and education to those seeking a greater understanding of their spiritual nature. Judith's work assists people to integrate harmony in the body, which creates freedom, inner peace and empowerment. She cherishes the opportunity to share her life experiences, to inspire and motivate people to believe in themselves and their dreams, thereby experiencing the JOY of life.

Judith is a spiritual mentor. She is a mother and a grandmother who has recently been on a "journey" following the guidance of her soul and Spirit traveling all through Canada, the United States and Mexico. Incorporating her years as a dance teacher, she has been referred to as "The Dancing Channel – the ONE voice of many."

Go to: **http://www.judithonley.com**

to order the Mp3s of the telechannels.